Poaching, Wildlife Trafficking and Security in Africa

Myths and Realities

Edited by Cathy Haenlein and M L R Smith

A joint publication from RUSI and King's College London's Marjan Centre for the Study of War and the Non-Human Sphere

www.rusi.org

Royal United Services Institute for Defence and Security Studies

Poaching, Wildlife Trafficking and Security in Africa: Myths and Realities
Edited by Cathy Haenlein and M L R Smith

First published 2016

Whitehall Papers series

Series Editor: Professor Malcolm Chalmers
Editor: Dr Emma De Angelis

RUSI is a Registered Charity (No. 210639)
ISBN 978-1-138-74377-9

Published on behalf of the Royal United Services Institute for Defence and Security Studies
by
Routledge Journals, an imprint of Taylor & Francis, 4 Park Square, Milton Park, Abingdon OX14 4RN

Cover Image: Guards from the Kenya Wildlife Service protect pyres of elephant tusks in Nairobi National Park in preparation for an ivory burn, April 2016. *Courtesy of Alamy/ Alissa Everett.*

SUBSCRIPTIONS
Please send subscription orders to:

USA/Canada: Taylor & Francis Inc., Journals Department, 530 Walnut Street, Suite 850, Philadelphia, PA 19106, USA

UK/Rest of World: Routledge Journals, T&F Customer Services, T&F Informa UK Ltd, Sheepen Place, Colchester, Essex CO3 3LP, UK

Contents

About the Editors

Cathy Haenlein is a Research Fellow in RUSI's National Security and Resilience Studies group, where she leads research on environmental crime. She is also a Research Associate at King's College London's Marjan Centre for the Study of War and the Non-Human Sphere, where she lectures on wildlife trafficking and its intersections with other forms of criminality. Cathy's research focuses on East Africa: she has conducted fieldwork on wildlife trafficking, illegal fishing and other forms of organised crime in Kenya, Tanzania, Uganda, Madagascar and the Seychelles. Cathy previously worked for various international NGOs, including as a Project Development Specialist based in Madagascar, focusing on environmental programmes.

Professor M L R Smith is Professor of Strategic Theory and Head of the Department of War Studies at King's College London. He is co-founder and Academic Director of the Marjan Centre for the Study of War and the Non-Human Sphere at King's College London. He has a particular interest in the impact of warfare on animals. Among his recent publications on this topic are: 'War and Wildlife: The Clausewitz Connection', *International Affairs* (Vol. 87, No. 1, 2011) (with Jasper Humphreys); 'Of Warriors, Poachers and Peacekeepers: Protecting Wildlife After Conflict', *Cooperation and Conflict* (Vol. 48, No. 4, 2013) (with Saskia Rotshuizen); and 'The "Rhinofication" of South African Security', *International Affairs* (Vol. 90, No. 4, 2014) (with Jasper Humphreys).

About the Authors

Stéphane Crayne is a consultant on wildlife protection strategies in Central Africa and is currently Chief Technical Advisor in the Okapi Wildlife Reserve in northeastern Democratic Republic of the Congo. Combining fieldwork and theory, he is also a Research Associate at the Marjan Centre for the Study of War and the Non-Human Sphere, King's College London. As a former French army officer and adviser to the WWF in the Central African Republic, he fosters a multidisciplinary approach to conservation in conflict zones, specialising in providing technical support to protected area management, as well as anti-poaching and security.

Professor Rosaleen Duffy is Professor of International Politics at the University of Sheffield. Her research focuses on the politics of conservation, wildlife trafficking, poaching, transfrontier conservation and ecotourism. Her most recent books include *Nature Crime: How We're Getting Conservation Wrong* (Yale University Press, 2010) and *Nature Unbound: Conservation, Capitalism and the Future of Protected Areas* (Earthscan, 2008) (with Dan Brockington and James Igoe). In September 2016, Rosaleen initiated a four-year, €1.8-million research project entitled 'Biodiversity and Security: Understanding Environmental Crime, Illegal Wildlife Trade and Threat Finance', funded by the European Research Council.

Jasper Humphreys is Director of External Relations at the Marjan Centre for the Study of War and the Non-Human Sphere, King's College London. He has published extensively on strategic issues relating to poaching and wildlife trafficking, following a BA in War Studies (2010) as a mature student. Recent publications have included 'War and Wildlife: The Clausewitz Connection', *International Affairs* (Vol. 87, No. 1, 2011) and 'The "Rhinofication" of South African Security', *International Affairs* (Vol. 90, No. 4, 2014) (both with M L R Smith). Hitherto, Jasper was a journalist, working for various British national newspapers as a general reporter.

Dr Thomas Maguire is a Junior Research Fellow at Darwin College and the Department of Politics and International Studies, University of Cambridge.

He is also a Project Coordinator and Research Associate at the Department of War Studies, King's College London. In 2014–15, Tom was a Visiting Fellow at RUSI, where he led a year-long research project examining connections between ivory trafficking, organised crime and terrorist financing in East Africa. He has published widely on this and other issues, including the influence of intelligence, interrogation and propaganda on counter-insurgency and the place of intelligence and propaganda in British and American Cold War statecraft.

Professor Keith Somerville is a Senior Research Fellow at the Institute of Commonwealth Studies and teaches at the Centre for Journalism, University of Kent. He is currently researching the nature and effects of human–wildlife conflict in Africa and the history of South African radio propaganda under Apartheid. His book *Ivory: Power and Poaching in Africa*, on the history and political economy of the ivory trade in Africa, was published by Hurst in November 2016. Keith's previous books include *Africa's Long Road since Independence: The Many Histories of a Continent* (Hurst, 2016) and *Radio Propaganda and the Broadcasting of Hatred* (Palgrave Macmillan, 2012).

Dr Tim Wittig is a scholar-practitioner, author and educator in the fields of illicit trafficking and finance. He is currently Senior Wildlife Trafficking Analyst with the Wildlife Conservation Society, and has previously worked for the US Department of Defense, US National Defense University, Johns Hopkins University and the University of Amsterdam. He is the author of numerous publications, including *Understanding Terrorist Finance* (Palgrave Macmillan, 2011).

Acknowledgements

This Whitehall Paper forms part of a joint initiative between RUSI and King's College London's Marjan Centre for the Study of War and the Non-Human Sphere. The aim of the collaboration is to bring together experts in the pursuit of a deeper understanding of the security dimensions of poaching and wildlife trafficking. This study is the first output of that partnership, and is the result of extensive research across source and transit countries in Africa by the authors in their respective areas of expertise.

The editors extend their gratitude to a number of people who have generously given their time and expertise in helping both to get this initiative off the ground and to facilitate the research and writing of this Whitehall Paper. They would especially like to thank Jasper Humphreys of the Marjan Centre, and Caroline Soper of the Marjan Centre and Chatham House, for their resolute support, astute advice and intellectual contributions over the course of the project. The editors would also like to thank RUSI Deputy Director-General Malcolm Chalmers, as well as Adrian Johnson and Emma De Angelis, former and current Directors of RUSI Publications, for their extensive analytical and practical support in the publication of this Whitehall Paper.

The editors would also like to thank the expert peer reviewers who contributed valuable comments at successive stages in the paper's development. In particular, they would like to thank John M Sellar OBE, independent anti-smuggling, fraud and organised crime consultant; Tanya Wyatt, Associate Professor/Reader in Criminology at Northumbria University; Tim Wittig and Hugo Rainey of the Wildlife Conservation Society; and Ledio Cakaj, independent researcher in conflict and armed groups. Finally, thanks are due to Ashlee Godwin, Edward Mortimer, Charlie de Rivaz and Sarah Hudson for their invaluable editorial input and efforts to ensure the smooth running of the production process. Ultimate responsibility for the content of this Whitehall Paper lies with the editors and authors alone.

INTRODUCTION

CATHY HAENLEIN AND M L R SMITH

Our planet is experiencing alarming levels of biodiversity loss. At present, experts estimate species loss to occur at around 1,000 times the natural extinction rate – the rate at which extinctions would take place if humans were not around.[1] Indeed, this crisis, unlike previous mass-extinction events, appears almost wholly the work of a single species: humankind. As a result of man's work, the world is witnessing the most intensive spate of species die-offs since the extinction of the dinosaurs 65 million years ago. The situation, as it stands, constitutes nothing less than a global environmental catastrophe.[2]

Poaching and wildlife trafficking are among the most immediate contributors to this disaster, alongside climate change, deforestation and habitat destruction. Today, wildlife (both dead and alive) is bought and sold on a vast scale for food, pets, skins, medicine, trophies and ornaments.[3] In wildlife consumer states, specialised markets operate at ever-greater levels of intensity; booming demand has triggered spikes in prices and thus in profits for those involved in the trade. The financial rewards on offer have in turn triggered devastating and unsustainable hunting. Serious poaching incidents are now more frequent, occur in previously untouched areas, and involve more advanced weaponry. Concurrently, the trafficking of poached wildlife has grown more sophisticated; networked criminal actors have entered the market,

---

[1] Jurriaan M De Vos et al., 'Estimating the Normal Background Rate of Species Extinction', *Conservation Biology* (Vol. 29, No. 2, April 2015).

[2] Adam Vaughan, 'Humans Creating Sixth Great Extinction of Animal Species, Say Scientists', *The Guardian*, 19 June 2015; WWF, *Living Planet Report 2014: Species and Spaces, People and Places* (Geneva: WWF, 2014).

[3] Elizabeth Bennett et al., 'Hunting the World's Wildlife into Extinction', *Oryx* (Vol. 36, No. 4, 2002).

facilitating the sourcing, transportation and onward sale of wildlife products across borders on an industrial scale.[4]

The harm this illicit activity causes is conventionally viewed in terms of the threat posed to affected species, and the risk of mass extinctions, with all of their wider biodiversity implications. Yet as the scale and profitability of wildlife trafficking have grown, the subject has begun to attract attention beyond the conservation community. This has occurred with rising fears over the dangers posed not just to wildlife, but also to the security and wellbeing of human populations. In November 2012, the US's then Secretary of State Hillary Clinton referred to wildlife trafficking for the first time as a critical national security issue.[5] The same year, the US Senate's Committee on Foreign Relations held a hearing on 'Ivory and Insecurity: The Global Implications of Poaching in Africa'.[6] John Kerry, then the chairman of the committee, opened the event with the observation that if poaching and wildlife trafficking continued unabated, it would bring 'more insecurity, more violence, ... and ultimately the degradation of stability of whole regions'.[7]

Written evidence submitted to the committee by Tom Cardamone of Global Financial Integrity described wildlife trafficking as posing 'serious national security concerns for the United States and our partners'.[8] The following year, UN Secretary-General Ban Ki-moon observed that poaching amounted to 'a grave menace to sustainable peace and security', in reference to the situation in Central Africa.[9] The NGO International Fund for Animal Welfare (IFAW) has described poaching and wildlife trafficking more broadly as 'no longer only a conservation or animal welfare issue[, but] ... a national and global security issue'.[10] The

4 UN Office on Drugs and Crime (UNODC), *World Wildlife Crime Report: Trafficking in Protected Species, 2016* (New York, NY: UN, 2016).

5 US Department of State, 'Remarks at the Partnership Meeting on Wildlife Trafficking', speech given by US Secretary of State Hillary Rodham Clinton, 8 November 2012, Washington, DC, <http://www.state.gov/secretary/20092013clinton/rm/2012/11/200294.htm>, accessed 5 May 2016.

6 US Senate Committee on Foreign Relations, 'Ivory and Insecurity: The Global Implications of Poaching in Africa', 112th Congress, Second Session, 24 May 2012, Washington, DC, <https://www.gpo.gov/fdsys/pkg/CHRG-112shrg76689/pdf/CHRG-112shrg76689.pdf>, accessed 25 April 2016.

7 *Ibid.*, pp. 2–3.

8 *Ibid.*, p. 16.

9 UN Security Council, 'Report of the Secretary-General on the Activities of the United Nations Regional Office for Central Africa and on the Lord's Resistance Army-affected Areas', S/2013/297, 2013, p. 15, para 74.

10 Marina Ratchford, Beth Allgood and Paul Todd, *Criminal Nature: The Global Security Implications of the Illegal Wildlife Trade* (Yarmouth Port, MA: International Fund for Animal Welfare, 2013), p. 7.

conclusion of World Bank environmental scientist Valerie Hickey is that 'the fight to end wildlife crime is a fight for humanity'.[11]

These statements offer striking appraisals of the threat posed by poaching and wildlife trafficking to human populations. Yet what has been largely missing is an elaboration on both the precise nature of the security threat posed and the evidence supporting such appraisals. Where such elaboration does occur, there is often a lack of coherence in the principal security narratives proffered. Poaching and wildlife trafficking are labelled simultaneously as drivers of conflict, market openings for organised criminals, and facilitators of terrorism – often without reference to concrete cases in point. Journalists, politicians and researchers have reiterated these threats, often without concern for the underlying evidence. As they have done so, key narratives have become self-sustaining, accepted as self-evident truths without regard for their basis in reality.

This worrying trend reflects a lack to date of detailed empirical research and analysis specifically on the security dimensions of poaching and wildlife trafficking. This is perhaps symptomatic of the earlier tendency to view poaching and wildlife trafficking as issues for conservationists, rather than as serious crimes falling within the purview of law enforcement and other security professionals.[12] The result is a growing acceptance of the new industrial-scale poaching and wildlife trafficking as a security threat without sufficient clarity on the type of poaching and wildlife trafficking posing the threat; the individuals and groups who pose this threat; or the communities whose security is threatened. It is the purpose of this Whitehall Paper to address these gaps, delving into the most common narratives and assessing their basis in reality.

Defining Poaching and Wildlife Trafficking

Such an analysis depends first and foremost on a clear understanding of what is meant by poaching and wildlife trafficking. This is not a straightforward matter: a range of terms is used to describe these processes, including wildlife crime and illegal wildlife trade. Organisations frequently use these terms interchangeably without clearly defining their scope.[13] The majority of references remain vague and subject to varying interpretations. Moreover, neither wildlife trafficking, nor wildlife crime,

---

[11] *Ibid.*, p. 11.

[12] WWF and Dalberg, 'Fighting Illicit Wildlife Trafficking: A Consultation with Governments', December 2012.

[13] WWF, 'Overview', <http://www.worldwildlife.org/threats/illegal-wildlife-trade>, accessed 1 September 2016.

nor illegal wildlife trade, are defined in any treaty. As a result, the international community continues to lack a common understanding or universally accepted definition that encompasses all forms of wildlife trafficked illegally, let alone a universal strategy to address the issue.[14] This is the case despite calls by the UN Environment Programme (UNEP) in 2014 for clarification, at UN level, on how illegal trade in wildlife should be conceptualised[15] – calls echoed by other individuals and organisations.[16]

As such, interpretations of the range of activities and commodities encompassed by poaching and wildlife trafficking are inconsistent. Some agencies use the term 'illegal wildlife trade' to cover 'the gamut from illegal logging of protected forests to supply the demand for exotic woods, to the illegal fishing of endangered marine life for food, and the poaching of elephants to supply the demand for ivory'.[17] Others distinguish between terrestrial species, aquatic species and timber. UNEP, INTERPOL and a range of other organisations have described 'illegal trade and poaching of wildlife and plants' as one of five major types of environmental crime, distinct from illegal logging and deforestation, illegal fishing, illegal mining and trade in minerals, and illegal dumping of toxic waste.[18] By contrast, the International Consortium on Combating Wildlife Crime – a collaboration between five intergovernmental organisations to protect natural resources – describes 'wildlife crime' in reference to 'all fauna and flora'. It describes fauna as 'animals and birds, such as tigers and falcons, but also ... fish' and flora as 'plants, such as orchids or cacti, but also ... timber and non-timber forest products'.[19]

---

[14] UNODC, 'Wildlife and Forest Crime Analytic Toolkit', revised edition, November 2012.

[15] Elisabeth McLellan et al., 'Illicit Wildlife Trafficking: An Environmental, Economic and Social Issue', UN Environment Programme Perspectives No. 14, May 2014.

[16] See, for example, Angus Nurse, *Policing Wildlife: Perspectives on the Enforcement of Wildlife Legislation* (Basingstoke: Palgrave Macmillan, 2015), pp. 13–40.

[17] US Fish and Wildlife Service, 'Illegal Wildlife Trade', <https://www.fws.gov/international/travel-and-trade/illegal-wildlife-trade.html>, accessed 5 May 2016.

[18] Christian Nellemann et al. (eds), *The Rise of Environmental Crime – A Growing Threat to Natural Resources, Peace, Development and Security* (Nairobi: UNEP and RHIPTO Rapid Response – Norwegian Center for Global Analyses, 2016), p. 30; Christian Nellemann et al. (eds), *Elephants in the Dust: The African Elephant Crisis* (Arendal: GRID-Arendal, 2013), p. 57.

[19] Convention on International Trade in Endangered Species of Wild Fauna and Flora (CITES), 'Wildlife Crime', <https://cites.org/prog/iccwc.php/Wildlife-Crime>, accessed 1 September 2016.

What makes trade in wildlife and wildlife products 'illegal' is a similarly complex issue.[20] The wildlife trade monitoring network TRAFFIC defines *any* form of wildlife trade, legal or illegal, as 'sale or exchange of wild animal and plant resources by people'.[21] This may include 'live animals and plants or a diverse range of products needed or prized by humans – including skins, medicinal ingredients, tourist curios, timber, fish and other food products'.[22] More specifically, under the Convention on International Trade in Endangered Species of Wild Fauna and Flora (CITES) – the principal global framework to regulate international trade in protected species – only trade that does not threaten species survival is allowed. CITES accords differing degrees of protection to around 35,600 species of wild animals and plants, whether traded alive or in dead parts.[23]

As an international treaty, CITES provides the international legal basis for signatory parties to operate in a common manner. Yet it ultimately depends on the implementation of consistent national legislation, which varies significantly among signatories.[24] Many of the 182 parties to CITES do not comprehensively criminalise activities involved in unsustainable trade in wildlife, and have not enacted specific national laws to implement the Convention.[25] Instead, they may rely on general wildlife and forest laws or on foreign-trade legislation not fully compliant with CITES.[26] Trade in a particular species can thus be legal in one country and illegal under CITES; or, conversely, it can be prohibited under national legislation and permitted under CITES.

This Whitehall Paper views 'illegal' trade in wildlife as that which violates either international legal frameworks or the national legislation of

---

20 Steven Broad, Teresa Mulliken and Dilys Roe, 'The Nature and Extent of Legal and Illegal Trade in Wildlife', in Sara Oldfield (ed.), *Trade in Wildlife: Regulation for Conservation* (Abingdon: Earthscan, 2003).

21 TRAFFIC, 'Background', <http://www.traffic.org/trade/>, accessed 5 May 2016.

22 *Ibid.*

23 CITES, 'Checklist of CITES Species', <http://checklist.cites.org/#/en>, accessed 5 May 2016. The Convention contains three separate appendices of species, and sets out the control mechanisms applicable to them. Appendix I includes species threatened with extinction in which commercial trade is not permitted. Appendix II includes species not necessarily in danger of extinction but which may become endangered if trade is not strictly regulated, and which can thus be traded only under a permit system. Appendix III includes species protected by national legislation established by the country that added them to the CITES list.

24 Vanda Felbab-Brown, 'The Disappearing Act: The Illicit Trade in Wildlife in Asia', Foreign Policy at Brookings Working Paper No. 6, June 2011, p. 4. It should also be noted that CITES is one of the few international conventions that can be supported by the application of sanctions.

25 UNODC, 'Wildlife and Forest Crime Analytic Toolkit', pp. 13–16.

26 *Ibid.*

affected countries, thus encompassing both domestic law and CITES regulations.[27] Rather than wildlife crime or illegal wildlife trade, it uses the terms 'poaching' and 'wildlife trafficking', to distinguish the illegal taking (poaching) of CITES-protected wildlife in source areas from activities involved in the illegal trade (trafficking) of these products. Given the limited scope of this study, the paper restricts its focus to a narrower definition of poaching and wildlife trafficking. This is understood as the illegal taking and trade in wild species of flora and fauna, excluding illegal fishing and logging.[28] In today's poaching and wildlife trafficking crisis, this covers a variety of species, from the lesser-known pangolin to iconic land mammals such as elephants and rhinos. However, it is the latter upon which this paper, in light of its focus on security threats, will principally concentrate.

Quantifying Poaching and Wildlife Trafficking

An analysis of the security dimensions of poaching and wildlife trafficking depends similarly on a clear understanding of the scale on which these processes occur. However, such an understanding is impeded by the clandestine nature of the practices involved. Many estimates have been ventured, but few with reference to a clear methodology. One of the most commonly cited estimations of illegal trade in flora and fauna (excluding fishing and logging), put forth by UNEP and INTERPOL, places the trade's value at anywhere between $7–23 billion per annum.[29]

Yet this figure is not broken down into its constituent parts, making the value of illegal trade in different species unclear. There is also no explanation of the uncertainty that gives rise to the notable difference in the upper and lower values of the estimate range. Meanwhile, other estimations of the trade's value have been made, from

[27] This is in line with the International Consortium on Combating Wildlife Crime's interpretation of wildlife crime as both 'acts committed contrary to national laws and regulations intended to protect natural resources and to administer their management and use' and, at the international level, 'violations of the Convention on International Trade in Endangered Species of Wild Fauna and Flora'. See CITES, 'Wildlife Crime'.

[28] There is, however, a strong need for a similar study of the security dimensions of illegal fishing and logging.

[29] Christian Nellemann et al. (eds), *The Environmental Crime Crisis – Threats to Sustainable Development from Illegal Exploitation and Trade in Wildlife and Forest Resources.* (Nairobi and Arendal: UNEP and GRID-Arendal, 2014), p. 19.

$5–20 billion in 2008,[30] to $7.8–10 billion in 2011,[31] and $7–10 billion in 2012.[32] In 2016, UNEP and INTERPOL once again estimated the value of illegal trade in flora and fauna to be $7–23 billion, despite reporting significant rises in other forms of environmental crime. They did so noting that no new estimate is available and that 'hence [the] original estimate is kept but needs revision'.[33]

By way of context, broader conceptions of illegal trade in wildlife that include illegal fishing and logging are affected by similar challenges. Here, again, perhaps the most widely used estimate is one published by UNEP and INTERPOL, which posit a substantially larger $70–213 billion.[34] This range was put forth in 2014, and was updated to a figure of $91–258 billion in 2016, amounting, UNEP and INTERPOL note, to an annual rise of 5–7 per cent.[35] This is frequently equated to the fourth-largest global form of illicit activity after drug trafficking, counterfeit crimes and human trafficking.[36] For the purposes of comparison, in 2016, UNEP and INTERPOL estimated annual values for these latter crime types at $344 billion, $288 billion and $157 billion respectively.[37]

The $91–258 billion figure again comprises a wide uncertainty range, attributed by UNEP and INTERPOL to the lack of criminal statistics available. Other estimations, meanwhile, differ substantially. In 2012, the OECD put the combined value of illegal trade in wildlife; illegal logging and its associated timber trade; illegal, unreported and unregulated fishing; illegal trade in controlled chemicals; and illegal disposal of hazardous waste, altogether, at a substantially smaller $30–70 billion per year.[38] In 2011, the US National Intelligence Council calculated that environmental crime – including illegal wildlife trade, logging, trade in chlorofluorocarbons (CFCs), and toxic waste dumping – generated an estimated $20–40 billion annually.[39]

---

[30] Liana Sun Wyler and Pervaze A Sheikh, 'International Illegal Trade in Wildlife: Threats and U.S. Policy', Congressional Research Service Report for Congress, RL34395, 22 August 2008, p. 2.
[31] Jeremy Haken, 'Transnational Crime in the Developing World', Global Financial Integrity, February 2011, p. 11.
[32] US Department of State, 'Secretary Clinton Hosts Wildlife Trafficking and Conservation', media note, 8 November 2012.
[33] Nellemann et al. (eds), *The Rise of Environmental Crime*, p. 20.
[34] Nellemann et al. (eds), *The Environmental Crime Crisis*, p. 7.
[35] Nellemann et al. (eds), *The Rise of Environmental Crime*, p. 7.
[36] *Ibid.*, p. 7.
[37] *Ibid.*, p. 21.
[38] OECD, 'Illegal Trade in Environmentally Sensitive Goods', October 2012, p. 2.
[39] See Office of the Director of National Intelligence, 'The Threat to U.S. National Security Posed by Transnational Organized Crime', special report, 2011.

In the case of both narrower and wider definitions, variations in estimates highlight the challenge inherent in quantifying wildlife trafficking. UNEP and INTERPOL, for example, acknowledge the existence of 'great uncertainties ... regarding the accuracy of the estimates'.[40] UNODC's 2016 *World Wildlife Crime Report*, meanwhile, abstains from specifying a figure at all, describing it as 'nearly impossible to give an accurate and consistent estimate of the criminal revenues generated by wildlife trafficking'.[41]

In line with this, independent anti-smuggling consultant John Sellar explores the issue of inadequate data collection and analysis in many affected countries. He notes that 'relatively few countries specifically collect data relating to wildlife trafficking', and that while some countries 'have some relevant data in, for instance, their central Customs seizure records[, they] ... may not seek to treat or analyse it as a distinct crime-type'. As a result, Sellar observes that 'the supply of such data to relevant IGOs [intergovernmental organisations] tends to be somewhat haphazard and incomplete'.[42] Only adding to this are the problems of distinguishing retail from wholesale values; variations in prices and profits along the trafficking chain; high levels of volatility in the seizure record; and speculation in high-value products due to year-on-year variations in prices and import volumes.[43]

Similar difficulties apply in calculating the *volumes* of wildlife products trafficked. These include a lack of investigative capacity and comprehensive data collection in many affected countries. Sellar highlights issues with some of the main monitoring systems, including a lack of consistent reporting by national customs authorities to the World Customs Organization and thus limitations to the latter's Central Enforcement Network. He observes a similar lack of reporting by national authorities to INTERPOL, impeding efforts to collate data on seizures or arrests.[44] As Sellar concludes, 'it seems reasonable to state that there is, at present, no meaningful or accurate overview of wildlife trafficking whatsoever'.[45]

---

[40] Nellemann et al. (eds), *The Environmental Crime Crisis*, p. 19.
[41] UNODC, *World Wildlife Crime Report*, p. 21.
[42] John M Sellar, 'Policing the Trafficking of Wildlife: Is There Anything to Learn from Law Enforcement Responses to Drug and Firearms Trafficking?', Global Initiative Against Transnational Organized Crime, February 2014, p. 15, <http://beta.stoprhinopoaching.org/UploadedFiles/Knowledge/Global%20Initiative%20-%20Wildlife%20Trafficking%20Law%20Enforcement%20-%20Feb%202014.pdf>, accessed 18 October 2016.
[43] UNODC, *World Wildlife Crime Report*, pp. 20–21.
[44] Sellar, 'Policing the Trafficking of Wildlife', pp. 15–16.
[45] *Ibid.*, p. 16.

A better overview exists for particular aspects of wildlife trafficking. Sellar acknowledges the greater volume of data available on ivory, for instance.[46] In this case, CITES monitors both poaching and trafficking via two systems: the Monitoring the Illegal Killing of Elephants (MIKE) system and the Elephant Trade Information System (ETIS) (although both are affected by limitations). Evidence from these mechanisms points to a major upsurge in elephant poaching and ivory trafficking from the mid-2000s, and particularly this decade.[47] A detailed study by Wittemyer et al. estimates that between 2010 and 2012 some 100,000 elephants were killed in Africa to feed the demand for ivory.[48]

Tanzania, Mozambique and parts of Central Africa have become the focus of this new wave of poaching and ivory trafficking.[49] In Tanzania, a government census revealed a 60 per cent drop in elephant numbers, from an estimated 109,000 in 2009 to just over 43,000 in 2014.[50] Fiona Maisels et al. have shown a decline of 62 per cent in forest elephants in Central Africa between 2002 and 2011.[51] Across Africa as a whole, elephant populations today are close to their lowest recorded level. In 2016, the International Union for Conservation of Nature's (IUCN) Species Survival Commission's African Elephant Specialist Group put elephant numbers at approximately 415,000.[52] This is estimated to amount to a net decline of 104,000–114,000 since 2007.[53]

Data on rhino-horn poaching and trafficking, meanwhile, show a trade that has spiralled out of control since 2007. Africa's rhino population is now a fraction of what it once was. Today, white rhino populations are

---

46 *Ibid.*

47 CITES, 'New Figures Reveal Poaching for the Illegal Ivory Trade Could Wipe Out a Fifth of Africa's Elephants over Next Decade', 2 December 2013.

48 George Wittemyer et al., 'Illegal Killing for Ivory Drives Global Decline in African Elephants', *PNAS* (Vol. 111, No. 36, 2014).

49 Samuel K Wasser et al., 'Genetic Assignment of Large Seizures of Elephant Ivory Reveals Africa's Major Poaching Hotspots', *Science* (Vol. 349, No. 6243, 2015), pp. 84–87.

50 Great Elephant Census, 'Better Data for A Crisis: Second Tanzania Count Part of Ongoing Population Monitoring', 9 September 2015; Karl Mathiesen, 'Tanzania Elephant Population Declined by 60% in Five Years, Census Reveals', *The Guardian*, 2 June 2015.

51 Fiona Maisels et al., 'Devastating Decline of Forest Elephants in Central Africa', *PLOS One*, 4 March 2013.

52 The study observed the possible existence of an additional 117,127–135,384 elephants in areas not systematically surveyed.

53 See C R Thouless et al., *African Elephant Status Report 2016: An Update from the African Elephant Database*, Occasional Paper Series of the International Union for Conservation of Nature Species Survival Commission, No. 60 (Gland, Switzerland: IUCN, 2016).

estimated at 19,682–21,077 and black rhinos at 5,042–5,455, according to the IUCN Species Survival Commission's African Rhino Specialist Group.[54] South Africa – home to the vast majority of white rhinos and around 40 per cent of black rhinos[55] – has suffered the most dramatic losses. Here, recorded numbers poached increased from 13 in 2007 to 122 in 2009, 448 in 2011, up to a peak of 1,215 in 2014.[56] Poaching and a lack of conservation have already caused the permanent disappearance of Africa's Western black rhino. The Northern white rhino, meanwhile, teeters on the verge of extinction as its three remaining individuals age.[57]

There is less data available on many of Africa's lesser-known species. Trade in pangolins, for example, has been regulated since 1975, with the entire genus added in 1994 to CITES Appendix II – which requires trade to be regulated through a permit system. Yet rising demand, predominantly in China and Vietnam, for pangolin meat and scales has raised concerns about the effectiveness of this protection.[58] This has come alongside rising seizures of illegally traded pangolin.[59] Between 2007 and 2015, the database World WISE documented seizures of 20 metric tons of scales, equivalent to around 54,000 live pangolins.[60]

Meanwhile, UNODC's 2016 *World Wildlife Crime Report* outlines available information on a range of other species, including those trafficked live for the pet and zoo trades. Much of the capture and sale of wild-caught animals for these trades involves birds and reptiles whose populations are challenging to monitor. The report notes that trade in tropical fish for aquaria and freshwater turtles and tortoises involves millions of individual creatures per year. The share of these creatures

---

[54] International Union for Conservation of Nature, 'IUCN Reports Deepening Rhino Poaching Crisis in Africa', 9 March 2016.

[55] African Wildlife Foundation, 'Rhinoceros', <http://www.awf.org/wildlife-conservation/rhinoceros>, accessed 2 August 2016.

[56] Numbers dropped only slightly to 1,175 in 2015. Data from South African Department of Environmental Affairs, 2016. See South African Department of Environmental Affairs, 'Minister Edna Molewa Highlights Progress in the Fight against Rhino Poaching', 21 January 2016.

[57] John R Platt, 'Northern White Rhino Dies, Leaving Just Three on the Planet', Extinction Countdown blog, *ScientificAmerican.com*, 22 November 2015; Matthew Knight, 'Western Black Rhino Declared Extinct', *CNN*, 6 November 2013.

[58] Demand in China and Vietnam relates to consumption both as food and for medicinal purposes. Pangolins also have significant cultural and historical uses in parts of Africa. For instance, the discovery and capture of a pangolin in some Mozambican provinces is seen as an indication of good luck and can elicit considerable celebration.

[59] Cathy Taibbi, 'Update on U.S. Fueling Pangolin Extinction', *Examiner.com*, 30 March 2016.

[60] UNODC, *World Wildlife Crime Report*, pp. 66–68.

which come from the wild, and are illegally sourced and traded, is difficult to ascertain.[61] Similarly challenging to monitor is the live trade in parrots including, notably, the African grey parrot from equatorial Africa. Building on a long history of export-quota violation, fraudulent declarations in CITES permit applications, and misdeclaration of captive breeding, this species has seen a large seizure volume relative to legal trade in recent years. This suggests a highly criminalised market rooted in Central Africa. In 2010, the export quota for wild-sourced African greys was 9,000 birds, with as many as 2,701 birds seized, according to World WISE records.[62]

The Development of Today's Crisis

Before delving into the security dimensions of the current poaching and wildlife trafficking crisis, it is worth pausing briefly to consider how this situation came about. Indeed, this crisis cannot be understood – nor effective solutions designed – without a nuanced understanding of how it developed. Yet such an account is again limited by a lack of reliable data, not least on little-known species for which comprehensive recording mechanisms have only recently been set up. More historical information is available, however, on two of the highest-value and most consistently sought-after wildlife products: ivory and rhino horn.

Trade in these two commodities has been documented for many centuries. In the case of ivory, there is evidence of trade between sub-Saharan Africa and North Africa, the Mediterranean, the Middle East and Asia as early as the first millennium BC.[63] Overseas demand for ivory grew with the ongoing expansion in long-distance trade, starting with Omani Arab and Indian trading along the East African coast. Demand expanded further from the late fifteenth century with the start of trading voyages by Europeans.[64] As this occurred, ivory became a source of great wealth along the coasts of East and West/Central Africa. This led, notably, to the rise of Zanzibar-based ivory traders able to exercise political and commercial hegemony across large parts of East and Central Africa.[65]

---

[61] *Ibid.*, pp. 73–76, referencing UN Comtrade and CITES trade data.

[62] *Ibid.*, pp. 76–81.

[63] Keith Somerville, *Ivory: Power and Poaching in Africa* (London: Hurst, 2016), pp. 9–24. Somerville also notes that the relationship between humans and elephants began long before this, with man hunting animals for meat and hides. There is evidence of the use of ivory for tools and fashion ornaments from between 25,000 and 35,000 years ago.

[64] *Ibid.*

[65] Alastair Hazell, *The Last Slave Market: Dr John Kirk and the Struggle to End the East African Slave Trade* (London: Constable, 2012).

As time wore on, the availability of more powerful weaponry and a substantial growth in ivory usage initiated a long-term decline in elephant numbers.[66] Demand rose steadily throughout the eighteenth and nineteenth centuries, but it was only in the twentieth century that falling elephant numbers began to attract real concern. Losses were often blamed by European settlers on African poaching rather than on Western sport hunting or global demand.[67] As such, the period from the end of the Second World War to independence from the late 1950s onwards saw the establishment of national parks, stricter regulation and the first militarised anti-poaching campaigns. Local people were not consulted, but simply ordered by colonial authorities out of the new protected areas.[68] From the late 1950s, meanwhile, few post-independence governments were concerned with wildlife management, occupied instead mainly with political consolidation and economic development.[69] At least at first, they made few significant changes to the running of the parks, conservation or hunting laws – with independence meaning little in terms of local empowerment.[70]

Rising poaching levels through the 1950s and 1960s eventually grew in the 1970s into a crisis driven by increasing demand for ivory in expanding economies like China and Japan. From a price in the 1960s of $5 per kg, ivory prices per kilogram rose, according to research by the academic Keith Somerville, to $7.50 in 1970, $74 in 1978, $120 in 1987 and $300 in 1987.[71] The 1980s saw the situation begin to spiral out of control. The African elephant population was estimated in 1979 at around 1.3 million in 37 range states; by 1989, only 600,000 remained.[72] This prompted the adoption of a ban on international ivory trade in 1989 as CITES listed African elephants on Appendix I (the highest level of protection, prohibiting all trade). As the ban came into force, poaching fell

---

[66] Somerville, *Ivory*, pp. 9–24.

[67] *Ibid.*

[68] *Ibid.*, pp. 57–59: in Kenya, for example, Nairobi National Park was gazetted in 1946, Tsavo in 1948 and Mount Kenya in 1949. In Uganda, Queen Elizabeth, Murchison Falls and Ruwenzori parks were set up in 1952 under the Uganda National Parks Act.

[69] Clark C Gibson, *Politicians and Poachers: The Political Economy of Wildlife Policy in Africa* (Cambridge: Cambridge University Press, 1999).

[70] Somerville, *Ivory*, p. 99; Ian Parker, *What I Tell You Three Times is True: Conservation, Ivory, History and Politics* (Kinloss: Librario Publishing, 2004).

[71] Somerville, *Ivory*, p. 103.

[72] Andrew M Lemieux and Ronald V Clarke, 'The International Ban on Ivory Sales and its Effects on Elephant Poaching in Africa', *British Journal of Criminology* (Vol. 49, No. 4, 2009).

dramatically and black-market ivory prices slumped. This allowed key elephant populations to recover or stabilise.

However, numerous attempts were made to weaken the ban. From the late 1990s these began to bear fruit. In 1999, CITES permitted Botswana, Namibia and Zimbabwe to make an 'experimental one-off sale' of almost 50 tonnes of ivory to Japan. In 2002, a further one off-sale was approved – this eventually took place in 2008 as 102 tonnes of ivory were sent to China and Japan.[73]

Many attribute today's renewed poaching and wildlife trafficking crisis directly to these one-off sales. They do so noting their impact on stimulating demand, while lamenting the ineffective safeguards on legal sales, which allow illegal ivory to be laundered into supplies labelled as legal.[74] Such a causal link is contested by scholars such as Daniel Stiles, who notes the fundamental difficulties – and, in his view, logical fallacies – associated with this argument.[75] While such debates rage, what is clear is that ivory trafficking has again spiralled out of control – in China, an increasingly affluent middle class had by 2014 driven wholesale prices to more than $2,000 per kg.[76] Such financial incentives and the scale of the poaching and ivory trafficking they have engendered mean that stemming this flow will entail responding to a situation of crisis proportions.

Trade in rhino horn has a similarly lengthy history. The Chinese were recorded as using rhino horn as medicine between 200 BC and 200 AD, and as carving horn into ornaments in the Ming and Qing dynasties.[77] In China and other parts of Asia and the Middle East, demand for rhino horn

---

73 CITES, 'Ivory Auctions Raise 15 Million USD for Elephant Conservation', press release, 7 November 2008.

74 Allan Thornton et al., 'Lethal Experiment: How the CITES-Approved Ivory Sale Led to Increased Elephant Poaching', Environmental Investigation Agency, April 2000; Damian Carrington, 'Legal Ivory Sale Drove Dramatic Increase in Elephant Poaching, Study Shows', *The Guardian*, 13 June 2016.

75 Daniel Stiles, 'CITES-Approved Ivory Sales and Elephant Poaching', *Pachyderm* (No. 45, July 2008–June 2009), pp. 150–52; Erwin H Bulte, Richard Damania and G Cornelis van Kooten, 'The Effects of One-off Ivory Sales on Elephant Mortality', *Journal of Wildlife Management* (Vol. 71, No. 2, April 2007), pp. 613–18.

76 Lucy Vigne and Esmond Martin, *China Faces a Conservation Challenge: The Expanding Elephant and Mammoth Ivory Trade in Beijing and Shanghai* (Nairobi and Lympne: Save the Elephants and the Aspinall Foundation, 2014). It must be noted, however, that ivory prices vary substantially depending on the size, quality and type of tusk; experts highlight distinctions particularly between forest elephant and savannah elephant tusks in terms of hue and density (and thus suitability for carving).

77 Nigel Leader-Williams, 'Regulation and Protection: Successes and Failures in Rhinoceros Conservation', in Oldfield (ed.), *The Trade in Wildlife*; Esmond and Chrysee Bradley Martin, *Run Rhino Run* (London: Chatto and Windus, 1982), p. 90.

expanded over time for use in a range of medicinal practices, as well as for dagger handles and other status symbols. By the twentieth century, and with the rise of the global conservation movement, unsustainable hunting had led to growing concern for rhinos' survival. Estimates suggest a global decline in all species of rhino from some hundreds of thousands in the early 1900s to perhaps 75,000 in the early 1970s.[78]

When CITES entered into force in 1975, rhinos were among the first species to be added to Appendices I and II. All species were moved to Appendix I by 1977. However, some countries were nevertheless allowed to continue to trade in live rhinos and to permit trophy hunting. Furthermore, whilst the ban prohibited international trade in theory, domestic sales in Asia remained legal and continued. Major consumer countries in the 1980s included China, Taiwan and South Korea, as well as Middle Eastern countries such as Yemen.[79]

Under these conditions, the ban at first largely failed to halt poaching.[80] Rhino populations declined as demand for their horns expanded further in the early 1990s. Between 1970 and 1995, the black rhino population dropped from 65,000 to just 2,410.[81] In response, from the early 1990s, international pressure and outcry intensified, and the international community took action to crack down on rhino horn sales. As a result, all major consumer countries brought in binding legislation to implement the CITES ban.[82]

For fifteen years, rhino populations in Africa began to recover: between 1990 and 2005, an average of just fourteen rhinos were poached in South Africa each year.[83] From the mid-2000s, however, poaching again began to rise. South Africa, as noted previously, has witnessed the most dramatic rise in poaching, with a record 1,215 rhinos poached in 2014,[84]

---

78 On declines in African rhinos over this period, see Richard Emslie and Martin Brooks, *African Rhino: Status Survey and Conservation Action Plan* (Gland and Cambridge: IUCN, 1999). On Asian rhinos over this period, see Thomas J Foose and Nico van Strien (eds), *Asian Rhinos: Status Survey and Conservation Action Plan* (Gland and Cambridge: IUCN, 1997).

79 WildAid, 'Rhino Horn Demand', pp. 1–3, <http://wildaid.org/sites/default/files/resources/WEBReportRhinoHornDemand2014.pdf>, accessed 1 August 2016; Katherine Ellis, 'Tackling the Demand for Rhino Horn', *The Horn* (Spring 2013), pp. 24–25.

80 Tom Milliken and Jo Shaw, *The South Africa–Viet Nam Rhino Horn Trade Nexus: A Deadly Combination of Institutional Lapses, Corrupt Wildlife Industry Professionals and Asian Crime Syndicates* (Johannesburg: TRAFFIC, 2012).

81 Emslie and Brooks, *African Rhino*, p. 5.

82 Ellis, 'Tackling the Demand for Rhino Horn'.

83 *Ibid*.

84 South African Department of Environmental Affairs, 'Minister Edna Molewa Highlights Progress in the Fight against Rhino Poaching'.

and with Vietnam emerging rapidly as the largest consumer of South African rhino horn.[85] Today, the price of rhino horn gives an idea of its value – and of the profits to be made. Some estimates put its value by weight at more than gold or cocaine in end markets: in 2012, it was estimated to be worth more than $65,000 per kg (although numerous difficulties affect this calculation).[86]

Poaching and Wildlife Trafficking as a Security Threat

The financial incentives offered by ivory, rhino horn and a range of other wildlife products have given rise to fears that these activities can have destabilising outcomes. Yet despite increasingly widespread acknowledgement of the potential threat, its true nature has not been examined as comprehensively as the risk to endangered species. The result has been the growth of a range of assumptions and poorly evidenced narratives on the security threat posed and the actors it involves.

The lack of detailed research into poaching and wildlife trafficking as a security threat stands in contrast to a rich field of study on broader conceptions of environmental security. This field emerged as a distinct strand of scholarship from the 1970s alongside shifting conceptions of 'security' itself (moving beyond state-on-state, military-centric paradigms towards a focus on the threats posed by transnational crime and terrorism).[87] Early environmental security research focused mainly on resource scarcity as a core component of non-military threats to security.[88] Yet as the debate matured after the end of the Cold War, further

---

85 For more detail on the emergence of Vietnam as a major destination market for rhino horn, see Environmental Investigation Agency, 'Vietnam's Illegal Rhino Horn Trade: Undermining the Effectiveness of CITES', February 2013; Julian Rademeyer, 'Vietnam Denies Rhino Horn Charges', *Mail & Guardian* (Africa), 15 March 2013; Milliken and Shaw, *The South Africa–Viet Nam Rhino Horn Trade Nexus*.

86 Michael 't Sas-Rolfes, 'The Rhino Poaching Crisis: A Market Analysis', Save the Rhino Trust, February 2012. Estimations vary: UNODC fieldwork at the end of 2015 has indicated a whole-horn retail price of about $26,000 per kg. For details of this estimate, see online methodological annex to UNODC, *World Wildlife Crime Report*, <https://www.unodc.org/documents/data-and-analysis/wildlife/Methodological_Annex_final.pdf>, accessed 18 October 2016.

87 Barry Buzan, Ole Wæver and Jaap de Wilde, *Security: A New Framework for Analysis* (London: Lynne Rienner Publishers, 1998); Richard A Matthew, Marl Halle and Jason Switzer (eds), *Conserving the Peace: Resources, Livelihoods and Security* (Winnipeg: International Institute for Sustainable Development, 2002); Jessica Tuchman Mathews, 'Redefining Security', *Foreign Affairs* (Vol. 68, No. 2, Spring 1989), pp. 162–77.

88 Richard A Matthew, 'The Environment as a National Security Issue', *Journal of Policy History* (Vol. 12, No. 1, 2000).

dimensions emerged. These included the threat posed by natural and polluting industrial disasters, and the dangers of human-induced climate change and other gradual changes to the environment.[89]

Poaching and wildlife trafficking have never received focused attention within this field of study, despite the views of many scholars that environmental security has expanded so far as to have become a 'vague and stretched concept'.[90] Meanwhile, outside the academic community, prior to the current spike in poaching and wildlife trafficking, these activities have rarely been discussed as security threats.[91] This is the case despite earlier poaching and wildlife trafficking disasters, such as the elephant-poaching crisis of the 1970s and 1980s, which involved both state and armed non-state actors.[92]

In this sense, the recent years of the current crisis have been very different. Most notably, they have witnessed a stream of strong rhetoric, particularly on wildlife as a driver of conflict and a funder of terrorism. Scenarios of heavily armed poaching gangs or bush-based terrorist groups poaching to finance their violence have characterised reporting on ivory poaching and trafficking. This rhetoric, however, is rarely grounded in evidence, in the examination of concrete cases; it is more often based on circular references or generalisations.

Purpose and Structure of this Whitehall Paper

This paper breaks down the rhetoric surrounding poaching and wildlife trafficking to assess its basis in empirical evidence. In doing so, it seeks to clarify how poaching and wildlife trafficking, as much-cited threats to security, can most accurately be conceived – an attempt to go beyond the generalisations in common usage. Such a study is crucial to efforts

---

[89] Geoffrey Dabelko, Steve Lonergan and Richard Matthew, 'State-of-the-Art Review on Environment, Security and Development Co-operation', report for the Working Party on Development Co-operation and Environment, OECD Development Assistance Committee; Matthew, Halle and Switzer, *Conserving the Peace*.

[90] Ashok Swain, 'Environmental Security: Cleaning the Concept', *Peace and Security* (Vol. 29, December 1997), p. 32; Dabelko, Lonergan and Matthew, 'State-of-the-Art Review on Environment, Security and Development Co-operation'.

[91] Katherine Lawson and Alex Vines, *Global Impacts of the Illegal Wildlife Trade: The Costs of Crime, Insecurity and Institutional Erosion* (London: Chatham House, February 2014).

[92] This crisis saw a reduction in Africa's elephant population of more than half, from 1.3 million to 600,000 between 1979 and 1989, eventually leading to the passage by CITES of the international commercial ban on ivory trade in 1989, which resulted for a time in a decline in poaching and the recovery of elephant populations. See Born Free, 'The Ivory Trade', <http://www.bornfree.org.uk/animals/african-elephants/projects/ivory-trade/>, accessed 18 September 2016.

by a range of stakeholders – from governments to NGOs and intergovernmental organisations – to respond to the security dimensions of poaching and wildlife trafficking. Misdiagnoses of the threat can skew responses in a way that not only fails to address the problem, but can also divert attention and funding from where they are most urgently needed.

As such, the focus of the paper is on identifying tension points between what is known and what is assumed to be known about the problem, and thus what can and should be done.[93] Interrogating such tension points is a useful analytic technique to identify the most effective modes of intervention in complex, multilayered problems. Unresolved divergences between public perception and observed reality can undermine not only the effectiveness of strategies against wildlife traffickers, but also the public and political will required for such strategies to succeed over the longer term.

Some aspects of the poaching–wildlife trafficking–security nexus have been analysed in greater detail than others. However, empirical research to date has usually had a micro focus, for example, on the extent to which a particular set of actors in a particular location may be benefiting.[94] What has been missing is a systematic evaluation of the different strands of evidence as part of a larger attempt to clarify how poaching and wildlife trafficking as broadly accepted security threats can most accurately be conceived.

In seeking to provide such an evaluation, this paper adopts a multilevel definition of security, moving beyond national security towards a broader conception that includes economic, societal and environmental security issues – at both the state and individual levels.[95] This conception aligns with a definition outlined by the OECD's Development Assistance Committee, which states that 'the security of people and the security of the State are mutually reinforcing', combined in 'an all-encompassing condition in which people and communities live in freedom, peace and safety, participate fully in the governance of their countries, enjoy the protection of fundamental rights, have access to resources and basic

---

[93] In social science, such 'tension points' are defined as 'power relations that are particularly susceptible to problematisation and thus to change, because they are fraught with dubious practices, contestable knowledge, and potential conflict'. See Bent Flyvbjerg, Todd Landman and Sanford Schram (eds), *Real Social Science: Applied Phronesis* (Cambridge: Cambridge University Press, 2012), Kindle edition, p. 288.

[94] Ledio Cakaj, 'Tusk Wars: Inside the LRA and the Bloody Business of Ivory', The Enough Project, 26 October 2015.

[95] Ashok Swain, *Understanding Emerging Security Challenges: Threats and Opportunities* (Abingdon: Routledge, 2013), pp. 14–16.

necessities of life, and inhabit an environment which is not detrimental to their health and well being'.[96] This approach to security views governance issues as central, insofar as state and non-state institutions have a role to play in protecting individuals. In this conception, security can be thought of as a 'public good', responding to the strategic need to promote sustainable development alongside national, regional and international stability. This understanding aligns in turn with moves to develop security paradigms within the African contexts on which this paper focuses. The African Union, for example, works on the basis of a 'multi-dimensional definition of security that encompasses both the traditional state-centric notion of the survival of the state and its protection from external aggression by military means, as well as the non-military notion of human security based on political, economic, social and environmental imperatives in addition to human rights'.[97]

Employing this understanding of security, this Whitehall Paper critically analyses four narratives that concern the nexus between poaching, wildlife trafficking and security: poaching and wildlife trafficking as threats to human security; poaching and wildlife trafficking as drivers of conflict; poaching and wildlife trafficking as funders of terrorism; and poaching and wildlife trafficking as a focus for organised crime. The Whitehall Paper examines these narratives whilst narrowing the focus to particular stages in the supply chain: to source and source/ transit countries in Africa. This choice is made in recognition of the highly differentiated processes involved across the full wildlife trafficking chain and the diverse political economies of the states affected, which also differ according to the wildlife derivative in question – and across which it is impossible to generalise.

The choice of geographic focus is also made in light of the fact that those individuals and states located closest to the point of the initial crime often experience the most critical harm. Indeed, it is in African source and source/transit areas that conceptualisations of merciless poaching gangs or of bush-based, ivory-funded militias – those that so frequently capture public imaginations – are most often based.[98] The chosen geographic

[96] OECD, *The DAC Guidelines: Helping Prevent Violent Conflict* (Paris: OECD, 2001), p. 38.

[97] See African Union, 'African Union Policy Framework on Security Sector Reform', 2013, p. 5, referencing African Union, 'Solemn Declaration on a Common African Defence and Security Policy', February 2004, p. 3, <http://www.peaceau.org/uploads/declaration-cadsp-en.pdf>, accessed 1 August 2016.

[98] See, for example, Horand Knaup and Jan Puhl, '"Blood Ivory": Brutal Elephant Slaughter Funds African Conflicts', *Spiegel Online*, 13 September 2012; Jeffrey Gettleman, 'Elephants Dying in Epic Frenzy as Ivory Fuels Wars and Profits', *New York Times*, 3 September 2012.

focus is thus logical: the African continent is a major source of many of the illegal wildlife derivatives circulating globally and witnesses many of the largest-scale and most aggressive poaching and anti-poaching actions.

With reference to these geographies, each of the four chapters examines a particular security narrative, following a consistent methodology to identify the relevant 'myths and realities' in each case. Each chapter starts with the findings of a rigorous review of secondary literature, analysed to reveal the dominant narratives and assumptions surrounding each element of the poaching–wildlife trafficking–security nexus. The review draws, in each case, on academic literature, policy documents, scientific data, publications by NGOs, research and advocacy groups, and news reporting, among other sources. Each chapter then critically analyses the *evidence* on which these understandings are based, highlighting misperceptions, myths and, by contrast, areas in which evidence provides clear support. This analysis is based on both primary and secondary research conducted over a number of years by the authors. Finally, the authors examine the practical implications of the myths and realities exposed, in terms of both how current understandings have affected responses, and the potential consequences for more nuanced responses.

Each chapter thus delves into a particular facet of the complex ecosystems of poaching, wildlife trafficking and security. In doing so, each seeks to break down narratives that are often highly generalised, omitting key considerations such as the commodity in question, the geographies affected, or the scale of the threat relative to others in the same regions. The aim is to deconstruct assertions of security trends that may be based on partial evidence, relevant only to particular species, locations or timeframes. An important aim throughout is to show how poaching and wildlife trafficking can be cited as security threats (often with reference to the above estimations of the billions generated) when in fact the most common and dramatic diagnoses – those on conflict and terrorism – relate to a single product: ivory (as explored in Chapters II and III). It is the purpose of this paper to uncover such inconsistencies, analysing the main wildlife–security themes according to their constituent parts.

Chapter I begins by examining the threat to human security and development nearest to the source of the commodities in question. The focus is on the full range of wildlife derivatives that may be poached and sold on in African source areas. There is a particular emphasis, however, on rhino poaching in southern Africa, in line with the authors' research. Here, the chapter considers the prevailing narratives on the threat posed to human security through the destruction of natural heritage of critical, long-term economic value. It argues that such understandings are partial, and that political and media narratives on poaching, wildlife trafficking and human security often fail to consider a range of other, more complex factors. These include the structural factors driving poaching in source areas, as well as the potential human impact of scaled-up anti-poaching enforcement responses.

Chapters II and III move on to examine a different genre of security threat. Going beyond Chapter I's focus on individual and community-level security, these chapters address the much-touted threat to state-level security deriving from understandings of poaching and wildlife trafficking as drivers of violent armed conflict and terrorism. Here, the paper divides the two chapters according to what are, in effect, two diverse facets of the public narrative. It examines, first, the extent to which poaching and wildlife trafficking sustain ongoing civil conflict (Chapter II), and, second, the degree to which they can fund terrorism (Chapter III). It does so acknowledging the overlaps that exist and the somewhat artificial nature of such a division, particularly given the often-inconsistent labelling of the groups involved in public statements. Both chapters, however, demonstrate the way in which ivory is conflated with wildlife more broadly: in both conflict and terrorism narratives, ivory is the commodity driving these assertions. It is thus solely ivory on which these two chapters focus.

Chapter II first seeks to situate ivory within the existing body of literature on conflict resources. It shows the limitations of current understandings of how ivory poaching and trafficking can fuel conflict. In the context of a lack of detailed case studies used to back up public statements, the chapter considers the case of the Central African Republic, on which the authors have conducted primary research. In particular, the authors analyse the prospects for nascent efforts to tackle poaching and wildlife trafficking in this context, as part of broader attempts to promote peace.

Linked to this, Chapter III examines myths and realities surrounding the much-publicised role of ivory poaching and trafficking in funding terrorist organisations. In seeking to critically analyse the basis for such assertions, the chapter examines existing evidence attesting to the involvement of actors commonly labelled 'terrorists' in poaching and ivory trafficking. The chapter focuses on the three most frequently cited groups: Al-Shabaab, the Lord's Resistance Army and the Janjaweed. In each case, it provides a more detailed assessment than is commonly proffered of the risk that ivory is bolstering these groups and their ambitions, and considers the implications for responses.

Chapter IV considers the individual and state-level threats posed by poaching and wildlife trafficking by examining dominant understandings of these activities as a form of organised crime. It argues that although the organised criminal nature of wildlife trafficking – as well as the corruption that accompanies it – is increasingly recognised, reflecting a solid body of evidence, the scale of the threat posed is less readily assessed. Here, the focus broadens out from ivory: organised crime penetrates trade in a range of species, from iconic pachyderms to the least-known species of reptile. The chapter argues further that knowledge gaps and misconceptions – on the degree of vertical integration of the organised crime groups involved, and the level of overlap with other forms of criminality – impede practical efforts to mitigate the threat. These tension points are studied with reference to primary research by the author in East Africa.

The paper concludes by drawing the analysis in each chapter into an overall picture of how poaching and wildlife trafficking as a security threat should most accurately be understood, on the basis of existing evidence. It argues that there is an imbalance in public narratives between a narrow focus on ivory as a driver of conflict and terrorism, and the more insidious threats posed to state cohesion, governance and human security by the organised crime and corruption driving poaching and wildlife trafficking more broadly. The paper argues that this focus must be inverted. It argues that much-touted insurgent and terrorist involvement in ivory poaching and trafficking comprises only one small part of the poaching and wildlife trafficking picture, rather than being indicative of an emerging trend or pervasive feature of it.

A holistic approach is thus needed, the paper maintains, to counter the different facets of security threat posed – at local, regional and state levels. This must form part of a multidimensional approach to address the threat facing both wildlife and human populations. Only through such an approach, based in evidence from African source and transit countries, can the impacts of this pernicious trade ultimately be addressed, both as they relate to the environment and as they concern our security.

I. POACHING, WILDLIFE TRAFFICKING AND HUMAN SECURITY

ROSALEEN DUFFY AND JASPER HUMPHREYS

Human security and underdevelopment are increasingly common themes in public debates about the security threat posed by poaching and wildlife trafficking. Most frequently highlighted are the ways in which these activities can exacerbate poverty by stripping local communities of the wildlife that tourists will pay to see. Such narratives, however, are oversimplified, underpinned by a series of assumptions about the circumstances and livelihoods of populations in source areas, and about the role of wildlife tourism in rural development. They do not adequately address the reasons poaching occurs in the first place, or the extent to which current responses to poaching themselves serve to ameliorate or threaten human security. This chapter examines the most common characterisations of the threat posed by poaching and wildlife trafficking to human security, questioning the extent to which they reflect available evidence of the range of threats that play out on the ground.

The Human Impact

Current understandings of the impact of poaching and wildlife trafficking on human security and development form part of a field of enquiry that is still developing. This field emerged in the late 1990s as part of a push to move beyond traditional, narrow definitions of national security that focused on states, without adequately addressing the security of 'people'.[1] Defining human security, for the purposes of this chapter, is far from easy;

[1] Karen O'Brien and Jon Barnett, 'Global Environmental Change and Human Security', *Annual Review of Environment and Resources* (Vol. 38, 2013), p. 373.

approaches to and understandings of the term often depend on the particular academic discipline or type of organisation (government, international organisation or NGO) using it.[2] However, a useful working definition is provided by Karen O'Brien and Jon Barnett in their extensive review of the debates on human security.

O'Brien and Barnett anchor the concept of human security in Amartya Sen's capabilities approach, which emphasises people's *aspirations* and how these can be met.[3] Aspirations, in Sen's analysis, encompass not only economics, but also power, voice and an ability to define one's own present and future. In line with this, O'Brien and Barnett suggest that human security is a condition in which people and communities have the capacity to respond to threats to their basic needs and rights so that they can live with dignity.[4] It is this broad understanding of human security that this chapter adopts.

Increasing attention to the intersections between human security and environmental change has resulted from the realisation that environmental degradation affects the ability of people to meet their basic needs and to live well. A similar trend has occurred in relation to poaching and wildlife trafficking specifically, with these activities now often suggested to have a straightforwardly negative impact on human security in and around source areas. It is assumed that this occurs as poaching removes the often-iconic wildlife that is key to tourism or community conservation schemes. These, it is emphasised, can form the only source of income in remote rural areas suffering high rates of poverty and a lack of access to other economic opportunities.

This argument forms a core part of calls to action by national governments in source and transit states, by development and conservation NGOs and by international organisations, as well as featuring frequently in mainstream media narratives. The 2014 London Conference on the Illegal Wildlife Trade – a conference that brought together global leaders with the aim of garnering high-level commitment to tackle wildlife trafficking – formally recognised the negative impact of poaching and

[2] There are substantial debates on security and human security. Useful overviews can be found in Astri Suhrke, 'Human Security and the Interests of States', *Security Dialogue* (Vol. 30, No. 3, 1999), pp. 265–76; Commission on Human Security, *Human Security Now: Protecting and Empowering People* (New York, NY: UN, 2003); Ken Booth, 'Security and Emancipation', *Review of International Studies* (Vol. 17, No. 4, October 1991), pp. 313–26; Richard A Matthew et al. (eds), *Global Environmental Change and Human Security* (Cambridge, MA: MIT Press, 2010); Ronnie D Lipschutz (ed.), *On Security* (New York, NY: Columbia University Press, 1995); Simon Dalby, *Security and Environmental Change* (Cambridge: Polity, 2009).

[3] Amartya Sen, *Development As Freedom* (Oxford: Oxford University Press, 1999).

[4] O'Brien and Barnett, 'Global Environmental Change and Human Security'.

wildlife trafficking on sustainable livelihoods. The resulting London Declaration describes wildlife trafficking as 'a major barrier to sustainable, inclusive and balanced economic development'.[5] The Declaration goes on to acknowledge the impact of wildlife trafficking on 'reduc[ing] … the revenue earned from economic activities such as wildlife-based tourism … which can make a significant contribution to local livelihoods and national economic development'.[6] This occurs, it notes, as wildlife trafficking 'robs States and communities of their natural capital and cultural heritage, … undermines the livelihoods of natural resource dependent communities … [and] damages the health of the ecosystems they depend on, undermining sustainable economic development'.[7]

The follow-up to the London Conference, held in Kasane, Botswana in 2015, emphasised that, 'As a result of illegal wildlife trade, communities lose the potential value of the resource that poachers and organised criminal networks are stealing from them', while also recognising that the impact on communities needed 'to be better understood and quantified'.[8] Meanwhile, proclaiming 3 March as World Wildlife Day in December 2013, the UN General Assembly reaffirmed 'the intrinsic value of wildlife and its various contributions, including ecological, genetic, social, economic, scientific, educational, cultural, recreational and aesthetic, to sustainable development and human well-being'.[9] Media content, where it considers the human impact of poaching and wildlife trafficking, focuses mainly on the loss of tourist revenues by dependent communities. The key points usually suggested are that, as a result of poaching and wildlife trafficking, 'sustainable employment opportunities for a poverty stricken population will be lost', as noted in an article on the situation in South Africa.[10] Numerous articles focus similarly on the point that 'The extinction of a species can have a negative economic effect on a local community's tourism industry. A community that relies on its wildlife to attract tourists is at great risk [of] … hardship if the prevalence of poaching is high'.[11]

---

[5] 'London Conference on the Illegal Wildlife Trade, 12–13 February 2014: Declaration', 2014, p. 8.

[6] *Ibid.*, p. 8.

[7] *Ibid.*, p. 2.

[8] 'Kasane Conference on the Illegal Wildlife Trade, 25 March 2015: Statement', 2015, pp. 6, 37, <https://www.gov.uk/government/uploads/system/uploads/attachment_data/file/417231/kasane-statement-150325.pdf>, accessed 15 July 2016.

[9] CITES, 'UN General Assembly Proclaims 3 March as World Wildlife Day', press release, 23 December 2013.

[10] *Fin24*, 'Rhino Poaching Threatens Tourism, Economy', 22 September 2013.

[11] Orietta C Estrada, 'The Devastating Effects of Wildlife Poaching', *One Green Planet*, 6 January 2014.

These assessments are not necessarily inaccurate. Poaching and wildlife trafficking can indeed impact upon human security in these ways. The hunting of wildlife through organised commercial poaching operations can remove an important resource for local communities. Wildlife may be part of community-based conservation schemes that generate important local revenues, in turn enhancing food security, and other forms of income and non-income security, in marginalised areas. A range of attempts has been made to illustrate the ramifications of this process, for example the iWorry campaign by the David Sheldrick Wildlife Trust. The campaign notes that in Kenya, wildlife tourism generates 12 per cent of GDP and 300,000 jobs, and raised $47 million in national park entrance fees in 2012 alone.[12] It then seeks to compare the value of a living versus a dead elephant, arguing that alive, a single elephant can contribute up to $22,966 to the tourism industry each year – around $1.6 million over its lifetime, compared to an average one-off total of $21,000 for its tusks (in end markets).[13]

However, there is also evidence to suggest that this characterisation does not represent the full picture. Although there is little published work on the reasons why people engage in illegal hunting and trafficking of wildlife, there is growing evidence to suggest that these practices can in fact have a *positive* impact on human security, making the situation more complex than the narrative cited above would suggest. This is precisely because proactive engagement in poaching and trafficking of a range of wildlife and wildlife products can itself meet subsistence needs or constitute an important source of income for some marginalised and vulnerable communities.[14] For example, forest-dependent peoples such as the Baka, Aka, Bagyeli, Bakola and Batwa in the Congo Basin have traditionally engaged in illegal hunting and fishing in protected areas to meet their protein needs.[15] Consumption of wildlife is critically important

---

[12] iWorry, 'Dead or Alive: Valuing an Elephant', 2014.

[13] *Ibid.*

[14] International Union for Conservation of Nature (IUCN) et al., 'Beyond Enforcement: Communities, Governance, Incentives and Sustainable Use in Combating Wildlife Crime', Symposium Report, 26–28 February 2015, Glenburn Lodge, Muldersdrift, South Africa, 2015; Catrina Mackenzie, Colin A Chapman and Raja Sengupta, 'Spatial Patterns of Illegal Resource Extraction in Kibale National Park, Uganda', *Environmental Conservation* (Vol. 39, No. 1, 2011), pp. 38–50.

[15] Aili Pyhälä, Ana Osuna Orozco and Simon Counsell, 'Protected Areas in the Congo Basin: Failing Both People and Biodiversity?', Rainforest Foundation UK, April 2016, pp. 80–81; Medard Twinamatsiko et al., *Linking Conservation, Equity and Poverty Alleviation: Understanding Profiles and Motivations of Resource Users and Local Perceptions of Governance at Bwindi Impenetrable National Park, Uganda* (London: IIED, 2014).

to their day-to-day survival, and increasing levels of enforcement are reported in the past to have led to malnutrition in some communities.[16] As Cooney et al. point out, poaching and wildlife trafficking can themselves be an important livelihood strategy.[17]

Meanwhile, poaching and wildlife trafficking can provide other benefits and respond to other motivations, beyond subsistence, on the part of local communities. These are often ignored in media and political narratives positioning poaching and wildlife trafficking as straightforward threats to development. Such narratives tend to rely on a narrow, predominantly economic definition of poverty; in a systematic review of evidence of the links between poverty and biodiversity, 70 per cent of published papers that addressed poverty as part of conservation used income as the key measure.[18] While poverty certainly encompasses material deprivation, it is necessary to engage with a much more complex understanding of the phenomenon.

Taking a human security approach, poverty is more than just a matter of economic deprivation; it encompasses concerns about status, the ability to shape one's own future, and to lead a dignified life. In light of O'Brien and Barnett's expansive understanding of poverty and human security,[19] it is important to consider whether poaching and wildlife trafficking might also be driven by a need to affirm identity or gain prestige.[20] In line with this, there is evidence to suggest that these activities may represent an act of resistance against rules that local communities regard as unfair or illegitimate.[21] Indeed, rarely considered in the dominant narratives around poaching, wildlife trafficking and human security is the fact that local communities may not agree with, nor wish to conform to, rules set by national governments, NGOs or international conservation initiatives.

---

16 See Pyhälä, Osuna Orozco and Counsell, 'Protected Areas in the Congo Basin', pp. 80–81; IUCN et al., 'Beyond Enforcement'.

17 R Cooney et al., 'The Trade in Wildlife: A Framework to Improve Biodiversity and Livelihood Outcomes', International Trade Centre (ITC), 22 May 2015; see also Dilys Roe et al. (eds), *Biodiversity Conservation and Poverty Alleviation: Exploring the Evidence for a Link* (Oxford: Wiley-Blackwell, 2013).

18 Roe et al., 'Which Components or Attributes of Biodiversity Influence Which Dimensions of Poverty?', *Environmental Evidence* (Vol. 3, No. 3, February 2014), p. 8.

19 O'Brien and Barnett, 'Global Environmental Change and Human Security'.

20 Rosaleen Duffy et al., 'Towards a New Understanding of the Links between Poverty and Illegal Wildlife Hunting', *Conservation Biology* (Vol. 30, No. 1, February 2016), pp. 14–22.

21 Rosaleen Duffy, 'Waging a War to Save Biodiversity: The Rise of Militarized Conservation', *International Affairs* (Vol. 90, No. 4, July 2014), pp. 828–29; John M MacKenzie, *Empire of Nature: Hunting, Conservation and British Imperialism* (Manchester: Manchester University Press, 1988).

The failure to examine the prevailing narratives more closely relates to the fact that such debates are often underpinned by a simple definition of poaching: namely, the hunting of any animal not permitted by the state or a private owner.[22] This is not a 'neutral' definition, however; it is one that is mainly informed and shaped by colonial histories. In sub-Saharan Africa, colonial authorities often outlawed hunting that used snares and traps, techniques used by communities to meet their subsistence needs.[23] While European sport hunters were portrayed as conservationists and respecters of wildlife, African hunting methods were presented as cruel and unsporting. Such images linked well with other colonial stereotypes of African communities as savage, uncivilised, barbaric and in need of European civilising missions,[24] with images of colonial sportsmen versus poachers still discernible in calls for militarised responses to poaching, as discussed later in this chapter.

These historical dynamics are reflected in many of the most common interpretations of subsistence versus commercial poaching today, even though hunting itself is difficult to categorise in neat and discrete ways. Subsistence poaching is often thought of as 'hunting for the pot', relying on basic technologies such as traps and snares, because the target is small game, such as antelope. By contrast, commercial poachers are typically thought to operate within organised groups that target financially valuable species such as elephants and rhinos. Commercial poachers, it is widely assumed, use superior technologies to hunt, including firearms, GPS systems and mobile phones.[25] However, increasingly these simple categories do not reflect the changing and dynamic nature of illegal hunting. Subsistence hunters may use automatic weapons, while commercial poachers may use traps and snares. For example, some forms of subsistence poaching have been transformed by the arrival of multinational mining and logging companies. In parts of Central and West

---

22 Duffy et al., 'Towards a New Understanding of the Links between Poverty and Illegal Wildlife Hunting', p. 15.

23 William M Adams, *Against Extinction: The Story of Conservation* (London: Earthscan, 2004), pp. 18–24; Duffy, 'Waging a War to Save Biodiversity'.

24 Roderick P Neumann, 'Moral and Discursive Geographies in the War for Biodiversity in Africa', *Political Geography* (Vol. 23, No. 7, 2004), p. 830; Adams, *Against Extinction*, pp. 331–41.

25 Rosaleen Duffy, *Nature Crime: How We're Getting Conservation Wrong* (New Haven, CT and London: Yale University Press, 2010), pp. 79–119. See also Twinamatsiko et al., *Linking Conservation, Equity and Poverty Alleviation*; Christian Nellemann et al. (eds), *The Environmental Crime Crisis – Threats to Sustainable Development from Illegal Exploitation and Trade in Wildlife and Forest Resources* (Nairobi and Arendal: GRID-Arendal, 2014); Mariel Harrison et al., *Wildlife Crime: A Review of the Evidence on Drivers and Impacts in Uganda* (London: IIED, 2015).

Africa, this has facilitated the growth of commercial bushmeat trading through the introduction of roads that allow the transportation of meat to urban markets or to meet the demand for food among large commercial workforces in remote rural areas.[26]

A number of cases point to the inadequacy of what are commonly viewed, at a policy level, as neutral definitions – and the failure to take account of local attitudes to them. Dilys Roe et al. demonstrate the centrality of poaching and wildlife trafficking to the livelihood strategies of some of the poorest communities in the world,[27] but argue also that these activities can represent more than a simple subsistence strategy. South Africa's rhino poaching crisis, for example, is often attributed to poverty in Mozambique, singled out as a 'problem state' at the sixteenth Conference of the Parties to CITES in 2013.[28] Mozambique remains one of the poorest countries in the world, despite the end of its long-running civil war in 1992. It shares a border with South Africa, one of the wealthiest countries on the continent, and is thought to constitute a major source of the poaching problem with poachers entering South Africa from Mozambique to acquire rhino horn that is then sold on to destination countries.

The available information suggests that the economic rewards of poaching here can be significant. A few days of work in Kruger National Park, which lies along Mozambique's western border with South Africa, can earn a Mozambican poacher between $1,000 and $5,000.[29] However, the argument that poverty alone drives Mozambicans to poach in South Africa ignores the wider political economy of poaching in the region. Mozambique's legislative framework, in particular, has contributed indirectly to poaching in South Africa because the penalties for involvement in poaching across the border have traditionally been minimal and the risks of being caught on return to Mozambique very low.

---

[26] For further discussion, see Kent H Redford, 'The Empty Forest', *BioScience* (Vol. 42, No. 6, 1992), pp. 412–22; Francis Massé and Elizabeth Lunstrum, 'Accumulation by Securitization: Commercial Poaching, Neoliberal Conservation and the Creation of New Wildlife Frontiers', *Geoforum* (Vol. 69, 2016), pp. 227–37; E J Milner-Gulland and N Leader-Williams, 'A Model of Incentives for the Illegal Exploitation of Black Rhinos and Elephants: Poaching Pays in Luangwa Valley, Zambia', *Journal of Applied Ecology* (Vol. 29, 1992), pp. 388–401; A Fischer et al., '(De) Legitimising Hunting – Discourses over the Morality of Hunting in Europe and Eastern Africa', *Land Use Policy* (Vol. 32, 2013), pp. 261–70.

[27] Roe et al., 'Which Components or Attributes of Biodiversity Influence which Dimensions of Poverty?', pp. 1–16.

[28] Rosaleen Duffy, Richard H Emslie and Michael H Knight, 'Rhino Poaching: How Do We Respond?', Evidence on Demand, October 2013, p. 6.

[29] Massé and Lunstrum, 'Accumulation by Securitization'.

Until the introduction of the country's 2014 Conservation Law, rhino-related offences such as possession of horn were considered as misdemeanours, not as crimes with associated penalties.[30] In addition, many of the communities on the Mozambique side of the border have a history of alienation from the parks, many of which encompass territories and resources to which they once enjoyed access. As a result, communities can regard poaching as a legitimate form of resistance to state authority.[31] In this case, poaching and wildlife trafficking cannot be explained as purely the result of economic deprivation.

Furthermore, a look back at the dynamics of elephant poaching during the crisis of the 1980s shows that even then poaching was not driven purely by poverty. In both East Africa in the 1980s and parts of southern Africa in the 1970s and 1980s, the large-scale poaching witnessed was not simply the result of poorer communities seeking to make a small amount of money from ivory in order to survive. Such organised levels of poaching could not have been carried out without corruption and complicity at the highest levels of government.[32] Indeed, the involvement of the former South African Defence Force (SADF) directly in poaching and wildlife trafficking was clearly exposed in the post-Apartheid report of the Kumleben Commission. The dedicated commission, headed by Mr Justice Kumleben and established in 1995, found that the SADF had used ivory, rhino horn, hardwoods and drugs to fund its wars and destabilisation campaigns in South West Africa (now Namibia), Angola and Mozambique.[33] The example of southern Africa in the 1980s is not unique, with extensive evidence also attesting to the high-level corruption behind today's poaching crisis (as explored in Chapter IV). In this context, it is crucial that poaching is not considered simply as a symptom of absolute poverty among communities living in proximity to protected areas.

---

[30] See Tom Milliken, Richard H Emslie and Bibhab Talukdar, 'African and Asian Rhinoceroses: Status, Conservation and Trade – A Report from the IUCN Species Survival Commission (IUCN/SSC) African and Asian Rhino Specialist Groups and TRAFFIC to the CITES Secretariat, Pursuant to Resolution Conf. 9.14 (Rev. CoP15) and Decision 14.89', CoP16 Doc. 54.2-rev 1, 2009, pp. 12, 18.

[31] Elizabeth Lunstrum, 'Green Militarization: Anti-Poaching Efforts and the Spatial Contours of Kruger National Park', *Annals of the Association of American Geographers* (Vol. 104, No. 4, 2014), pp. 816–32.

[32] Ros Reeve and Stephen Ellis, 'An Insider's Account of the South African Security Force's Role in the Ivory Trade', *Journal of Contemporary African Studies* (Vol. 13, No. 2, 1995), pp. 222–43.

[33] Stephen Ellis, 'Of Elephants and Men: Politics and Nature Conservation in South Africa', *Journal of South African Studies* (Vol. 20, No. 1, 1994), pp. 53–69; Reeve and Ellis, 'An Insider's Account of the South African Security Force's Role in the Ivory Trade'.

This latter consideration points to the need to consider involvement in wildlife trafficking, beyond the poaching stage. Particularly at the next stages along the chain, it is crucial to acknowledge that trafficking, and the corruption that accompanies it, can constitute a regular source of income for some, while for others, they represent a safety net or a lucrative business opportunity.[34] Here, it may be *relative* poverty that is more important as a driver, with individuals in many rural areas motivated by opportunities to acquire the levels of material wealth associated with inclusion in the global economy (expressed through ownership of consumer goods such as mobile phones, televisions and vehicles).[35] Although beyond the geographical focus of this paper, a 2008 report by TRAFFIC in relation to Asia made exactly this point, concluding that the recent increase in wildlife trafficking in Southeast Asia was not poverty related, but directly related to a rise in household incomes. This study examined different stages in the trafficking chain, from local-level rural harvesters to professional hunters, traders, wholesalers and retailers – categories that also apply in sub-Saharan Africa. Wildlife trafficking provided varying forms of economic benefits along different stages of the chain, constituting a source of regular income, a safety net or a profitable business venture.[36] Clearly, participation in wildlife trafficking at progressively higher stages of the chain to meet these expectations is different from that which occurs at the harvesting stage to meet the basic subsistence needs of local communities.

As such, even from this small sample of examples, it is clear that poaching, wildlife trafficking, development and human security are intertwined in more complex ways than the commonly invoked causal relationship would suggest. Indeed, the arguments positioning poaching as a straightforwardly negative force in relation to human security in source areas ignore the changing nature of these activities, the immediate livelihoods demands on certain communities, and the range of other interests they may hold. These considerations are crucial to evaluating both the adequacy of dominant narratives around the threat posed by poaching and wildlife trafficking to human security, and the effectiveness of policy responses. In source areas, these include a range of approaches, from those that seek to provide alternative livelihood options, to those that seek to

---

[34] TRAFFIC, 'What's Driving the Wildlife Trade? A Review of Expert Opinion on Economic and Social Drivers of the Wildlife Trade and Trade Control Efforts in Cambodia, Indonesia, Lao PDR and Vietnam', TRAFFIC International and World Bank, 2008, pp. ix–x, 59–60, 68; Roe et al. 'Which Components or Attributes of Biodiversity Influence which Dimensions of Poverty?'; Nellemann et al. (eds), *The Environmental Crime Crisis*, pp. 17–18.

[35] Daniel W S Challender and Douglas C MacMillan, 'Poaching is More than an Enforcement Problem', *Conservation Letters* (Vol. 7, No. 5, 2014), pp. 484–94.

[36] TRAFFIC, 'What's Driving the Wildlife Trade?', pp. 59–60, 68.

change the motivations and behaviours of poachers and members of local communities, and those that promote greater use of force in enforcement, regardless of the poacher's motivations.[37]

Policy Implications

Approaches focused on poverty alleviation and alternative livelihoods have increasingly been viewed as central to a range of responses to poaching and wildlife trafficking. These approaches align with a view of poaching and wildlife trafficking as threats to human security due to their destructive impact on natural heritage of critical economic and touristic value. They also respond to a view of poverty as the main cause of poaching and wildlife trafficking in source areas, the logical solution to which is to develop economic alternatives for would-be poachers and traffickers. As such, these responses seek to develop alternative income-generating options, through job creation and the disbursement of revenue from wildlife tourism schemes.[38]

This approach has underpinned initiatives such as Integrated Conservation and Development Projects – conservation projects that contain a rural development component – and, more recently, community conservation programmes that have a greater focus on development, such as CAMPFIRE in Zimbabwe and ADMADE in Zambia. Such programmes seek to understand and tackle the structural and contextual factors that drive poorer communities to engage in poaching and wildlife trafficking. However, they have been increasingly criticised for their lack of attention to the ways in which they intersect with existing community dynamics, often reinforcing hierarchies and failing to disburse benefits to the most marginalised and vulnerable community members.[39]

---

[37] Alternative approaches might include community-based natural resource management and demand reduction programmes for wildlife products. For an overview, see Wolfram H Dressler et al., 'From Hope to Crisis and Back Again? A Critical History of the Global CBNRM Narrative', *Environmental Conservation* (Vol. 37, No. 1, 2010), pp. 1–11; John Hutton, William M Adams and James C Murombedzi, 'Back to the Barriers? Changing Narratives in Biodiversity Conservation', *Forum for Development Studies* (Vol. 32, No. 2, 2005), pp. 341–70; Stuart A Marks, 'Back to the Future: Some Unintended Consequences of Zambia's Community-Based Wildlife Program (ADMADE)', *Africa Today* (Vol. 48, No. 1, 2001), pp. 120–41.

[38] Dilys Roe et al., 'Conservation and Human Rights: The Need for International Standards', IIED briefing, 2010; Christopher B Barrett and Peter Arcese, 'Are Integrated Conservation–Development Projects (ICDPs) Sustainable? On the Conservation of Large Mammals in sub-Saharan Africa', *World Development* (Vol. 23, No. 7, 1995), pp. 1073–84.

[39] Dressler et al., 'From Hope to Crisis and Back Again?'; Hutton, Adams and Murombedzi, 'Back to the Barriers?'; Marks, 'Back to the Future'.

Meanwhile, such approaches often remain anchored in a very narrow definition of poverty, conceived as a matter solely of economic deprivation. The result is that initiatives aiming to alleviate poverty or provide alternative livelihoods via income generation often have limited positive results – precisely because they fail to tackle wider problems of inequality, the historical processes that led to the establishment of poaching as a crime or, crucially, the wider aspirations of poorer communities. These factors need to be more fully considered and integrated into any efforts to change the behaviour of would-be poachers. This requires a very different policy approach: one that seeks to address the aspirations of communities, as well as engaging more fully with wider national and international development policies to reduce poverty and inequality.[40] Rather than narrowly focusing on developing new models for protected areas and wildlife management, such approaches should place wildlife management models within their broader social and political context.

A related policy response is to change the balance of risk and reward associated with poaching and wildlife trafficking. This response similarly rests on the idea that poachers, for example, exercise individual choice (or agency) in making the decision to hunt (or not to hunt).[41] It is often assumed that an individual chooses to engage in poaching because they have decided that the potential rewards – commonly conceived as a means of economic subsistence in a context of absolute poverty – outweigh the potential risks. According to this logic, tackling poaching becomes a matter of increasing the rewards on offer for refraining from this activity, or increasing the risks and costs associated with it.

In order to deter poachers, therefore, government and conservation agencies may seek to increase the benefits or rewards available in exchange for a reduction in poaching, such as direct payments or investment in community projects such as schools, water pumps or grinding mills, as in the case of both CAMPFIRE and ADMADE.[42]

---

[40] For further discussion, see Rosaleen Duffy et al., 'The Militarization of Anti-Poaching: Undermining Long Term Goals', *Environmental Conservation* (Vol. 42, No. 4, 2015), pp. 345–48.

[41] Freya A V St John, Gareth Edwards-Jones and Julia P G Jones, 'Conservation and Human Behaviour: Lessons from Social Psychology', *Wildlife Research* (Vol. 37, No. 8, 2010), pp. 658–67; Duffy et al., 'Towards a New Understanding of the Links between Poverty and Illegal Wildlife Hunting'.

[42] Aidan Keane et al., 'The Sleeping Policeman: Understanding Issues of Enforcement and Compliance in Conservation', *Animal Conservation* (Vol. 11, No. 2, 2008), pp. 75–82; Milner-Gulland and Leader-Williams, 'A Model of Incentives for the Illegal Exploitation of Black Rhinos and Elephants'; C A Litchfield, 'Rhino Poaching: Apply Conservation Psychology', *Science* (Vol. 340, No. 6137, 2013), pp. 1168.

Government and other agencies may also seek to increase the risks of detection, arrest and imprisonment, on the basis that greater levels of enforcement serve to encourage compliance with the law and deter participation in poaching.[43] Again, however, the effectiveness of such approaches depends on the extent to which poaching is conducted purely as a means of economic subsistence – meaning that schemes such as direct payments would be considered attractive. Where local communities regard rules around 'poaching' as illegitimate, however, the deterrent effect of increased rewards for abstinence – or greater penalties associated with participation in poaching – is likely to be limited.

A final policy option is to rely on an increased use of force to offer protection to wildlife populations from poachers, regardless of their reasons for involvement in this activity. The dramatic rise in poaching of elephants and rhinos for ivory and horn since the mid-2000s has prompted a more enthusiastic embrace of this option, commonly witnessed in a forceful enforcement response.[44] Such militarised forms of anti-poaching activity are not new: there is a long history of cooperation between the military and conservation sectors and the integration of conservation initiatives into security agendas; early game wardens in British colonial administrations were often ex-military personnel, for instance.[45] Today, this trend has reached new heights, as poachers have become more heavily armed, making greater use of sophisticated weaponry and technologies such as GPS, night-vision goggles and even helicopters.[46] As the militarised activities of poachers are matched by corresponding militarised responses, the result has increasingly been framed as an existential 'war for wildlife'.[47]

Many conservation agencies and supporters of military-style conservation point to the need for increased use of force in encounters with heavily armed poachers prepared to shoot to kill both animals and rangers that get in their way. Rangers can often encounter heavily armed poachers during patrols, and shots are regularly exchanged. This is demonstrated in the number of rangers killed during anti-poaching operations, even while carrying out routine duties associated with managing protected areas. The

---

[43] Duffy et al., 'Towards a New Understanding of the Links between Poverty and Illegal Wildlife Hunting'; Esmond Martin, 'Effective Law Enforcement in Ghana Reduces Elephant Poaching and Illegal Ivory Trade', *Pachyderm* (No. 48, 2010), pp. 24–32.

[44] Duffy et al., 'The Militarization of Anti-Poaching', pp. 345–48.

[45] Neumann, 'Moral and Discursive Geographies in the War for Biodiversity in Africa'.

[46] Duffy et al., 'The Militarization of Anti-Poaching'.

[47] David Smith, 'Africa is Centre of a "Wildlife War" That the World is Losing', *The Guardian*, 21 March 2015; Ranjeni Munusamy, 'Rhino Poaching: It's War!', *Daily Maverick*, 1 March 2013.

Thin Green Line Foundation, which campaigns on behalf of rangers killed or wounded on duty, estimates that 1,000 rangers have been killed worldwide in the last ten years while carrying out their duties.[48] This figure is likely an underestimate given the patchiness of data collection and reporting of rangers killed on duty in some countries.

In this context, it is widely accepted that a robustly armed contribution to conservation is indispensable. Researchers Jasper Humphreys and M L R Smith invoke Clausewitz, who wrote that 'if one side uses force without compunction, undeterred by the bloodshed it involves, while the other side refrains, the first will gain the upper hand'.[49] This logic has underpinned the rise of what has come to resemble a niche variant of counterinsurgency in ungoverned spaces. Nir Kalron, a former Israeli paratrooper who runs the environmental security firm Maisha Consulting's Wildlife Security Operations, sees his role as a holistic union of war and wildlife protection. He notes that his own professional 'transition from the Israeli Defense Forces to conservation was one of natural continuity; the standards and ethical code I was taught in the special operations teams and the sense of fighting for just causes were and still are the core values that guide me'.[50] Similarly, former Coldstream Guards officer Ian Saunders of the Tsavo Trust promotes the Stabilization through Conservation ('StabilCon') concept in Kenya. The objective of StabilCon is to enhance the physical security of wildlife and communities in at-risk areas by deploying professional anti-poaching units, trained to meet the specific challenges of their local area, which provide physical safety for both people and wildlife.[51]

The growing inclination towards militarised anti-poaching is unsurprising given the fractured political and security situation in parts of Africa; the heightened rhetoric around high-value wildlife such as elephants and rhinos; and the large numbers of former military personnel who have sought to bring their special brand of knowledge, honed in conflict zones such as Afghanistan, to wildlife conservation. However, as might be expected, these strategies have drawn criticism, especially from those who approach conservation as a development issue, as being too 'militarised', propagating 'green violence' and 'green militarisation'.[52] This

---

48 The Thin Green Line Foundation, 'Our Story', <https://www.thingreenline.org.au/story/>, accessed 11 October 2016.

49 Jasper Humphreys and M L R Smith, 'War and Wildlife: The Clausewitzian Connection', *International Affairs* (Vol. 87, No. 1, 2011).

50 Nir Kalron, 'Role of the Private Sector', *The Cipher Brief*, 30 November 2015.

51 Tzavo Conservation Group, 'Stabilization through Conservation (StabilCon)', <http://www.tsavocon.org/stabilcon/>, accessed 18 July 2016; Tanya Saunders, 'Opinion: Tourism Is Important, But It's Not the Only Reason to Save Elephants', A Voice for Elephants blog, *National Geographic*, 31 October 2014.

52 Lunstrum, 'Green Militarization'.

critique maintains that force is being applied within a militaristic process of 'weaponising' conservation, and that the construction of 'war' narratives around these issues is unhelpful. As researcher Elizabeth Lunstrum argues, more militarised responses produce increasingly dangerous landscapes as state actors, private operators and poachers enter into conservation areas willing to contribute with deadly force.[53] This, she notes, can result in an inevitable cycle of escalation, with limited or even counterproductive impacts, particularly on human security.[54]

Indeed, while the justifications for increased use of force rely on a 'self-defence' argument, some operations use force proactively and as a means of pre-emption – at times going as far as establishing policies of shoot-to-kill – rather than as a reaction to a distinct threat.[55] The impact on human security is often little considered; as Roe points out, communities can be negatively affected by heavy-handed militarised responses, which result in a proliferation of weapons and armed personnel in marginalised rural areas that may already be confronting insecurity. For example, the Democratic Republic of the Congo has experienced decades of military activity by a wide range of rebel groups and government forces; in this context, armed anti-poaching units may simply be regarded as yet another militia, estranging communities rather than giving them a stake in wildlife protection strategies.[56]

Indeed, whilst a militarised approach may result in a short-term reduction in poaching, it may ultimately undermine longer-term, community-based approaches.[57] This reflects the inability of militarised responses, alone, to engage with and tackle the complex social, political and economic contexts that produce illegal actions against wildlife in the first place. This can manifest itself in a failure to distinguish between poaching for profit and for subsistence,[58] involving a failure to acknowledge that poaching and wildlife trafficking are often orchestrated by organised criminal syndicates, sometimes through the co-option or coercion of hunters from poorer local communities, with additional negative effects on human security.[59] Alone, a militarised response

---

53 *Ibid.*; Rosaleen Duffy, 'War, by Conservation', *Geoforum* (Vol. 69, 2016), pp. 238–48.

54 Lunstrum, 'Green Militarization'.

55 Duffy, 'Waging a War to Save Biodiversity'.

56 Richard Milburn, 'Mainstreaming the Environment into Postwar Recovery: The Case for "Ecological Development"', *International Affairs* (Vol. 88, No. 5, 2012), pp. 1083–100.

57 Duffy et al., 'The Militarization of Anti-Poaching'.

58 Dilys Roe (ed.), 'Conservation, Crime and Communities: Case Studies of Efforts to Engage Local Communities in Tackling Illegal Wildlife Trade', IIED, 2015, p. 8.

59 Robert W Burn, Fiona M Underwood and Julian Blanc, 'Global Trends and Factors Associated with the Illegal Killing of Elephants: A Hierarchical Bayesian Analysis of Carcass Encounter Data', *PLOS One* (Vol. 6, No. 9, 2011).

ignores the key question of how governments and conservation groups can devise ways for the benefits of wildlife conservation to be delivered to local communities – questions that must be considered simultaneously.

Finally, it must be acknowledged that there may be more to narratives of 'war' and militarisation of anti-poaching than the imperatives of animal protection and ranger self-defence – with further impacts at community level. Indeed, securitising a topic is often seen to have two important effects: to make the issue a top priority for policymakers, and to make it one that demands urgent solutions, usually militarised ones.[60] These effects can at times suit vested interests, an issue raised in relation to the situation in South Africa, where the militarisation of poaching and anti-poaching has perhaps extended to its furthest point. Here, the militarisation of anti-poaching received a boost from 2012 when General (retired) Johan Jooste became head of anti-poaching in South Africa's national parks. He did so declaring his dismay that the country was 'under attack from armed foreign nationals' and stating his determination 'to take the war to these armed bandits and ... to win it'.[61]

This idealistic 'rhino wars' narrative, however, has been criticised as having been hijacked by a number of private interests. These relate to the fact that a significant proportion of South Africa's rhinos live on private farms and ranches,[62] providing a range of business opportunities for the South African farmer/rancher. South Africa is the only country (apart from Namibia, where a few permits are issued) to allow rhino hunting, providing a different motivation for an uncompromising approach to their protection.[63] Similarly, demand for rhino horn would present a potentially major financial opportunity for farmers/ranchers if international trade were to be legalised – again pointing to a different (financial) stimulus for militarised protection strategies. At the same time, South Africa's fight

[60] Roger Mac Ginty, 'Against Stabilization', *Stability* (Vol. 1, No. 1, 2012); Ashok Swain, 'Environmental Security: Cleaning the Concept', *Peace and Security* (Vol. 29, December 1997).

[61] South African National Parks, 'SANParks Enlists Retired Army General to Command Anti-Poaching', media release, 12 December 2012, <http://www.sanparks.org/about/news/default.php?id=55388>, accessed 12 June 2016.

[62] Michael H Knight, Richard H Emslie and R Smart (compilers), 'Biodiversity Management Plan for the White Rhinoceros (Diceros Bicornis) in South Africa 2013–2018', prepared by the SADC Rhino Management Group following a multistakeholder workshop at the request of the South African Minister of the Environment on behalf of the Department of Environmental Affairs, 2013; Shirley Brooks et al., 'Creating a Commodified Wilderness: Tourism, Private Game Farming, and "Third Nature" Landscapes in KwaZulu-Natal', *Tijdschrift voor Economische en Sociale Geografie* (Vol. 102, No. 3, 2011).

[63] David Bilchitz, 'Rhino Hunting is Not Compatible with Conservation', *Daily Maverick*, 14 March 2016.

against poaching has become big business for fundraising organisations synchronised with graphic television programmes such as *Battleground: Rhino Wars*,[64] and the already numerous private security companies that provide anti-poaching and de facto help to fill the rural security void.[65] These concerns have been outlined most forensically by journalist Julian Rademeyer, who points to the range of interlocking elements comprised by South Africa's 'rhino wars'.[66] These range, notably, from the protection of a high-profile animal (motivated by a variety of conservation, combat, political and economic considerations) to competition between different groups engaged in cynical and logistically complex strategies to cash in on a valuable resource.[67] In all of this, the impact on development and the security of populations in and around source areas is little considered.

In this context, it is clear that more effective and more socially just responses to the threat posed by poaching at the local level are required. These must be based on a more sophisticated understanding of how poaching and low-level wildlife trafficking can impact on human security. This must involve recognition that these activities may have positive as well as negative impacts on human security, in both the shorter and longer term. In cases where poaching is an important part of subsistence or income-generating strategies for poorer communities, policymakers must provide alternatives that genuinely address the *aspirations* of communities, rather than simply providing income or employment opportunities. They must also be aware of the potentially negative impacts of militarised responses to poaching and wildlife trafficking on human security. The ultimate risk is that these approaches alienate the very communities upon which successful, long-term conservation ultimately relies.

---

64 Animal Planet, *Battleground: Rhino Wars*, 19 February 2013, <http://animal.discovery.com/tv-shows/battleground-rhino-wars>, accessed 12 June 2016.

65 See, for example, Protrack Anti-Poaching Unit, <www.protrackapu.co.za>, accessed 12 June 2016. South Africa's private security sector is already the largest in the world, with some 9,000 registered businesses employing 400,000 registered security guards. See Victoria Eastwood, 'Bigger than the Army: South Africa's Private Security Forces', *CNN*, 8 February 2013.

66 Julian Rademeyer, *Killing for Profit: Exposing the Illegal Rhino Horn Trade* (Cape Town: Zebra Press, 2012).

67 Sharon Gilbert-Rivett, 'Legalising the Trade in Rhino Horn and a Wilderness of Greed', *Africa Geographic*, 4 December 2013; Julian Rademeyer, 'Tipping Point: Transnational Organised Crime and the "War" on Poaching', Global Initiative against Transnational Organized Crime, July 2016, pp. 48–55; Julian Rademeyer, 'The Crooks Behind Rhino Slaughter', *Financial Mail*, 15 July 2016.

II. POACHING, WILDLIFE TRAFFICKING AND CONFLICT

STÉPHANE CRAYNE AND CATHY HAENLEIN

Beyond the community level examined in Chapter I, one of today's core narratives around poaching, wildlife trafficking and security focuses on the threat to governments from wildlife-funded civil conflict. Indeed, although not all instances of armed conflict in Africa occur where wildlife is abundant, a range of examples shows what happens when they do. These range from the dwindling cheetah populations of the strife-torn Horn of Africa,[1] to the gorilla victims of eastern Democratic Republic of the Congo's (DRC) civil wars. All appear to be testament to a destructive nexus between wildlife, instability and violent conflict, where they coexist.[2]

This nexus has been much analysed in the field of environmental security. Yet most research into conflict, poaching and wildlife trafficking specifically has approached the issue from a single direction, focusing on the ways in which conflict can grant poachers and traffickers space in which to thrive. The inverse question – the way in which poaching and wildlife trafficking themselves drive and fund conflict – is often addressed only with recourse to generalisations, and without reference to grounded

---

1 Damian Carrington, 'Cheetah Smuggling Driving Wild Population to Extinction, Report Says', *The Guardian*, 15 July 2014; CITES, 'Sixty-Fifth Meeting of the Standing Committee Geneva (Switzerland), 7–11 July 2014: Interpretation and Implementation of the Convention Species Trade and Conservation: Illegal Trade in Cheetahs (Acinonyx Jubatus)', 2014, <https://www.cites.org/sites/default/files/eng/com/sc/65/E-SC65-39.pdf>, accessed 26 September 2015; p. 4.

2 Andrew J Plumptre et al., 'Support for Congolese Conservationists', *Science* (Vol. 288, No. 5466, 2000); Sarah Zielinski, 'Congo's Civil Wars Took a Toll On Its Forests', *Smithsonian.com*, 26 February 2014; G Vogel, 'Conflict in Congo Threatens Bonobos and Rare Gorillas', *Science* (Vol. 287, No. 5462, 2000).

evidence.[3] This chapter examines common characterisations of wildlife trafficking, and ivory trafficking in particular, as a force fuelling conflict, and questions the extent to which these characterisations reflect available evidence. It examines a case on which the authors have conducted extensive research – that of conflict and ivory trafficking in Central African Republic (CAR).

A Link Between Poaching, Wildlife Trafficking and Conflict?

In many African contexts, war is a killer for wildlife and the ecosystems on which it depends.[4] In many unstable areas, species suffer as a direct result of the often extreme violence and destruction born of human conflict. They can also suffer indirectly, as conflict disrupts governance, the rule of law and security, allowing poaching and wildlife trafficking to ramp up unchecked.[5] Indeed, these activities often thrive where conflict weakens centralised authorities, permitting the rise of corruption, informal shadow economies and alternative non-state structures.

In South Sudan, for instance, one of the largest untouched savannah and woodland ecosystems in Africa is threatened by ongoing civil war. In December 2013, two years after independence, conflict broke out between forces loyal to President Salva Kiir and those aligned with his former deputy, Riek Machar. Since then, unrestrained poaching has flourished; the wildlife service has reported the loss of at least 500 elephants as armed actors have proliferated, disrupting park management operations, and facilitating poaching and wildlife trafficking.[6] Boma National Park has been particularly hard hit; the killing of the park warden and wildlife officers and the looting of park headquarters in 2013 have further disrupted the park's ability to protect its animals.[7]

---

[3] There are a few exceptions. See Avi Brisman et al. (eds), *Environmental Crime and Social Conflict: Contemporary and Emerging Issues* (Abingdon: Routledge, 2015).

[4] Joseph P Dudley et al., 'Effects of War and Civil Strife on Wildlife and Wildlife Habitats', *Conservation Biology* (Vol. 16, No. 2, 2002); Thor Hanson et al., 'Warfare in Biodiversity Hotspots', *Conservation Biology* (Vol. 23, No. 3, 2009); Andrew Plumptre et al., *L'impact de la guerre civile sur la conservation des aires protégées au Rwanda* (Washington, DC: Biodiversity Support Program, 2001).

[5] Christian Nellemann et al. (eds), *Elephants in the Dust: The African Elephant Crisis* (Arendal: GRID-Arendal, 2013), p. 57; Richard A Matthew et al. (eds), *Conserving the Peace: Resources, Livelihoods and Security* (Winnipeg: International Institute for Sustainable Development, 2002).

[6] Okech Francis, 'South Sudan Says 500 Elephants May Have Died During Two-Year War', *Bloomberg*, 9 February 2016.

[7] Wildlife Conservation Society (WCS), 'Ongoing War Threatens Existence of Elephants and Other Key Wildlife Species in South Sudan', press release, 4 December 2014.

The effects have been monitored by the NGO Wildlife Conservation Society (WCS), which reported the poaching of some 30 per cent of satellite-collared elephants over the course of 2014.[8] By the end of the year, WCS reported elephant numbers in South Sudan to be down to just 2,500,[9] while the presence of tens of thousands of armed actors was reported to have contributed to a substantial increase in subsistence hunting. The country's giraffe and tiang antelope, among other animals, have been butchered to feed these actors.[10] Slow progress in implementing a peace deal continues to threaten their survival.[11]

Successive civil wars and ongoing instability in eastern DRC further demonstrate the ways in which the absence of an effective national authority, the proliferation of non-state armed actors and inward migration from an unstable neighbourhood can damage wildlife populations through an upsurge in poaching and wildlife trafficking.[12] Increasingly, however, concern has mounted over the inverse relationship: the extent to which the dynamics of poaching and wildlife trafficking can themselves influence the course of conflict in biodiversity-rich areas. Fears around this causal link have emerged alongside concern over a broader crime–conflict nexus, which sees armed non-state actors replace ideologically motivated financial support from external sources with the proceeds of criminal enterprise.[13] These fears have grown as the value of ivory in particular – and thus the potential risk of 'blood ivory' – has risen since the mid-2000s. It is ivory specifically that is viewed as the particular form of wildlife most capable of funding conflict, and the resource on which this chapter will focus.

The conceptualisation of ivory as a driver of conflict first received high-level attention in the early 2010s. Hillary Clinton, in her last weeks as US secretary of state in November 2012, stated publicly: 'we have good

---

[8] *Ibid.*

[9] *Radio Tamazuj* (Sudan), 'Elephant Herds Devastated in South Sudan Civil War: Report', 17 November 2014.

[10] Christina Russo, 'New Doubts About Whether Elephants Can Survive South Sudan's Civil War', *National Geographic*, 8 December 2014.

[11] James Butty, 'South Sudan's Riek Machar Calls for Armed Struggle', *Voice of America*, 26 September 2016.

[12] Plumptre et al., 'Support for Congolese Conservationists'; Jefferson S Hall et al., 'A Survey of Elephants (*Loxodonta africana*) in the Kahuzi-Biega National Park Lowland Sector and Adjacent Forest in Eastern Zaire', *African Journal of Ecology* (Vol. 35, No. 3, 1997); Curtis Abraham, 'Endangered Primates Caught in Congolese Conflict', *New Scientist*, 28 November 2012; Brian Clark Howard, 'Chief Warden Shot in Africa's Oldest National Park', *National Geographic*, 17 April 2014.

[13] See Chris Dishman, 'The Leaderless Nexus: When Crime and Terror Converge', *Studies in Conflict and Terrorism* (Vol. 28, No. 3, 2005); Ian Bannon and Paul Collier (eds), *Natural Resources and Violent Conflict: Options and Actions* (Washington, DC: World Bank, 2003).

reason to believe that rebel militias are players in a worldwide ivory market worth millions and millions of dollars a year'.[14] John Kerry's State Department took this line forward: in 2013, M Brooke Darby, deputy assistant secretary of state for the Bureau of International Narcotics and Law Enforcement Affairs, asserted that wildlife trafficking could 'feed militant groups, terrorist groups and other criminal activity'.[15] In 2013, the US National Intelligence Council published an open source study concluding that 'Criminal elements of all kinds, including some terrorist entities and rogue security personnel, ... are involved [... in wildlife trafficking] across east, central, and southern Africa'.[16] Two years later, on World Wildlife Day 2015, President of the UN General Assembly Sam Kahamba Kutesa noted further that rebel groups were playing an active part in the trafficking of wildlife.[17]

With these and numerous other formal statements, the argument that wildlife – used in many cases as an inaccurate synonym for ivory – funds conflict has become embedded in the public imagination.[18] This has occurred particularly as the media has embraced the narrative. To give just a few examples, in 2012, *Spiegel Online* spoke of 'blood ivory' as 'rebels and militias' across Africa discovered the illegal trade as a lucrative means to fund their wars.[19] In 2014, the *New Scientist* went so far as to suggest that the ivory trade 'funds most conflict and terrorism in Africa'.[20]

Common to many of these assertions is a generality born of an inadequate body of underlying empirical research. As such, there is a corresponding tendency to say little about the mechanisms through which the named armed actors benefit, the scale of their involvement or their importance as players, both relatively and absolutely, in the trade. The ivory–conflict narrative usually relies on generalities even when it comes

---

[14] US Department of State, 'Remarks at the Partnership Meeting on Wildlife Trafficking', speech given by US Secretary of State Hillary Rodham Clinton, Benjamin Franklin Room, Washington, DC, 8 November 2012, <http://www.state.gov/secretary/20092013clinton/rm/2012/11/200294.htm>, accessed 17 August 2015.

[15] Aggrey Mutambo, 'US State Department Links Poaching to Terrorism', *Daily Nation*, 15 November 2013; US National Intelligence Council (NIC), 'Wildlife Poaching Threatens Economic, Security Priorities in Africa', 6 September 2013.

[16] NIC, 'Wildlife Poaching Threatens Economic, Security Priorities in Africa'.

[17] UN General Assembly, 'Statement by the President at the Commemoration of World Wildlife Day', New York, NY, 4 March 2015, <http://www.un.org/pga/040315_statement-world-wildlife-day>, accessed 17 August 2015.

[18] Rosaleen Duffy, 'Al-Shabaab and Ivory (1)', Marjan Centre for the Study of War and the Non-Human Sphere, 26 September 2015.

[19] Horand Knaup and Jan Puhl, '"Blood Ivory": Brutal Elephant Slaughter Funds African Conflicts', *Spiegel Online*, 13 September 2012.

[20] Richard Schiffman, 'Ivory Poaching Funds Most War and Terrorism in Africa', *New Scientist*, 14 May 2014.

to the groups that are said to be benefiting. At best, these are indicated by passing references usually to the Séléka in CAR (examined in this chapter), Al-Shabaab in Somalia, or the Lord's Resistance Army (LRA) and Janjaweed across parts of Central Africa (examined in Chapter III in relation to claims around the funding of terrorism).[21] These references are often made without recourse to detailed empirical research to back them up.[22] Meanwhile, it can be unclear from public statements to which wildlife products they refer, speaking as they often do of 'illegal wildlife trade' or 'wildlife trafficking' without clarification as to whether this, in reality, extends beyond ivory.[23]

This generality is due, in part, to the fact that trafficking in wildlife derivatives such as ivory has not featured prominently in major works that comprise the academic literature since the 1990s on the role of natural resources in funding and sustaining violent conflict in Africa.[24] This literature notes the increasingly prominent role of natural resources in armed conflict, particularly following the end of the Cold War as belligerents came to rely more on commercial sources of funding than on ideological sponsorship.[25] The commercialisation of war economies gave rise to fears that wars were being waged for financial rather than political reasons, and that war profiteering was becoming a key dimension of protracted African conflicts.[26] As one of the most readily available sources of finance on the continent, easily extractable natural resources received most attention in this regard.

Many of the ensuing academic debates over 'greed versus grievance' in civil conflict focused on particular case studies – mainly the supposedly new-style, identity-driven and predatory wars of the immediate post-Cold War era.[27] These were typified by 'conflict diamonds' in Sierra Leone's

---

[21] See, for example, Liana Wyler and Pervaze A Sheikh, 'International Illegal Trade in Wildlife: Threats and U.S. Policy', Congressional Research Service, RL34395, July 2013, pp. 5–6.

[22] NIC, 'Wildlife Poaching Threatens Economic, Security Priorities in Africa'; UN General Assembly, 'Statement by the President at the Commemoration of World Wildlife Day'.

[23] *Ibid.*

[24] Philippe Le Billon, *Wars of Plunder: Conflicts, Profits and the Politics of Resources* (London: Hurst, 2012).

[25] I O Lesser, *Resources and Strategy: Vital Materials in International Conflict, 1600–The Present* (New York, NY: St Martin's Press, 1989); Mats Berdal and David M Malone (eds), *Greed and Grievance: Economic Agendas in Civil Wars* (Boulder, CO: Lynne Rienner Publishers, 2000).

[26] David Keen, *The Economic Functions of Violence in Civil Wars* (London: International Institute of Strategic Studies, 1998).

[27] Mary Kaldor, *New and Old Wars: Organised Violence in a Global Era* (Cambridge: Polity Press, 1999).

civil war of 1991–2002, and 'conflict minerals' during decades of warfare in eastern DRC.[28] Ivory and other wildlife products rarely featured in this literature, passed over amid the commotion over easily looted stones and minerals. This trend has, for the most part, continued. Ivory, for example, does not feature once in Philippe Le Billon's 2012 work on conflict resources, *Wars of Plunder*.[29]

This is the case despite evidence of involvement by armed groups in poaching and trafficking – particularly of ivory – even prior to the so-called 'new wars' era. In the 1980s, before the global ivory trade ban in 1989, rising demand and prices made ivory a commodity of high value to conflict actors.[30] Research has revealed that in the late 1970s, and 1980s, both the National Union for the Total Independence of Angola (UNITA) – then fighting for Angolan independence – and the Mozambican National Resistance (RENAMO) were heavily involved in the killing of elephants and trafficking of ivory.[31] There is also evidence of state collusion; both UNITA and RENAMO were able to export ivory through Pretoria, facilitated by elements in South Africa's special forces.[32] This occurred as ivory from Angola, for example, was taken into Namibia, where it received official veterinary stamps 'legalising' it, before it was sold to dealers in South Africa and exported as legal ivory.[33]

This activity is thought to have fed into a broader Apartheid South African strategy to destabilise 'frontline states' – newly independent, black majority-rule neighbouring states, including Angola and Mozambique from 1975, and Zimbabwe from 1980.[34] The destabilisation involved overt military intervention, the provision of arms and training to rebel movements, covert attacks and collusion with criminal elements. In the case of Namibia, collusion with criminal groups and front companies saw food and other support sent to UNITA and ivory, rhino horn and timber brought

---

[28] Paul Collier and Anke Hoeffler, 'Greed and Grievance in Civil War', World Bank Policy Research Working Paper No. 2355, May 2000.

[29] Le Billon, *Wars of Plunder*.

[30] Didrik Schanche, 'Ivory Price Rise Brings Surge in Elephant Slaughter', *Lawrence Journal World*, 25 May 1988.

[31] Ros Reeve and Stephen Ellis, 'An Insider's Account of the South African Security Forces' Role in the Ivory Trade', *Journal of Contemporary African Studies* (Vol. 13, No. 2, 1995).

[32] *Ibid.*; Graham Ferreira, 'SA's Part in Ivory Scandal', *Sunday Tribune* (Durban), 22 April 1984.

[33] Reeve and Ellis, 'An Insider's Account of the South African Security Forces' Role in the Ivory Trade'.

[34] *Ibid.*

out of UNITA-held territory.[35] Funds went to UNITA, to South African military intelligence and into the pockets of South African military and intelligence personnel, as recorded by Stephen Ellis in his extensive research.[36] There is evidence to suggest that many of those in South Africa's special forces had been professional hunters, game-park wardens or otherwise involved in the wildlife business before being trained in bush warfare. They helped UNITA and, in the case of Mozambique, RENAMO to establish and maintain efficient ivory-harvesting operations.[37] In both Mozambique and southeastern Zimbabwe – in Gonarezhou National Park, on the Mozambican border – large-scale poaching was facilitated by conflicts in both countries. Both the 1964–79 Zimbabwe War of Liberation and 1977–92 Mozambican civil war allowed poaching by insurgents and military units under the cover of insurgency and counterinsurgency operations.[38] This occurred particularly as Rhodesian special forces began conducting incursions into Mozambican to assist RENAMO and fight Zimbabwean guerrillas based there in the late 1970s.

Although these Cold War-era examples do not in themselves demonstrate a clear and direct role for poaching or ivory trafficking in funding conflict, they nonetheless show the complex intersections between conflict, poaching and ivory trafficking, and point to the need for further interrogation. Yet scholarly research today has for the most part continued to bypass ivory as a conflict resource.[39] Perhaps as a function of this, the kind of global architecture that has developed to prevent trade in more clearly recognised conflict resources such as diamonds has failed to materialise in the case of ivory and other wildlife products.[40] Certainly, the Convention on International Trade in Endangered Species of Wild

---

[35] *Ibid.*; authors' correspondence in May 2016 with Keith Somerville regarding interviews with Colonel Jan Breytenbach, commander of the South African Defence Force's 32 Battalion in southern Angola, November 1990.

[36] Authors' correspondence in May 2016 with Keith Somerville regarding interviews with Colonel Breytenbach, November 1990; with Stephen Ellis, December 2014; and with Anthony Turton, a former South African intelligence operative, April 2015. See also M B Kumleben, 'Commission of Inquiry into the Alleged Smuggling of and Illegal Trade in Ivory and Rhinoceros Horn in South Africa: Report of the Chairman, Mr Justice M B Kumleben Judge of Appeal', January 1996, p. 111.

[37] De Wet Potgieter, 'War Veteran Links SADF to Unita Ivory Slaughter', *Sunday Times* (Johannesburg), 19 November 1989.

[38] Keith Somerville, *Ivory: Power and Poaching in Africa* (London: Hurst, 2016), pp. 176–78.

[39] Exceptions which *do* touch upon ivory and conflict in this sense include R T Naylor, 'The Underworld of Ivory', *Crime, Law and Social Change* (Vol. 42, Nos. 4–5, January 2005).

[40] US Department of State, 'Conflict Diamonds', <http://www.state.gov/e/eb/tfs/tfc/diamonds/index.htm>, accessed 9 May 2016; Global Witness, 'The Dodd-Frank Act', 26 January 2015.

Fauna and Flora (CITES) has evolved into a comprehensive global mechanism to regulate trade in wildlife. However, this exists as an imperative of avoiding irreversible species loss rather than as a function of the need to deprive militant groups of funding.

All of this means that today's organised and industrial-scale ivory poaching and trafficking is frequently cited by politicians and the media as a source of funding for conflict without the institutional frameworks or systematic use of current research to substantiate such claims. In this context, the examination of a specific recent case study – that of CAR – is of particular value. The aim is to assess the extent to which evidence on the ground, in this particular case, supports the prevailing political and media narrative of a destabilising ivory–conflict connection. This complements the cases of Al-Shabaab, the Janjaweed and the LRA examined in Chapter III.

The Case of CAR

In May 2013, the world recoiled at images of the mass slaughter of 26 elephants in CAR's Dzanga Sangha Protected Areas (hereafter Dzanga Sangha). The killings occurred in Dzanga Bai, a world-famous watering hole known as the 'village of elephants', where hundreds of forest elephants would gather daily to drink mineral salts from the sands.[41] The event occurred at the height of CAR's civil war, coinciding with a surge of vicious factionalism between the mostly Muslim Séléka and Christian Anti-Balaka militias, just months after the former had seized power in the capital, Bangui.[42] The elephant massacre – notably the threat it signalled for an until-then relatively unscathed UNESCO World Heritage Site – made global headlines. It also prompted urgent calls for the international community to restore peace and order in CAR for the sake of both its citizens and its natural heritage.[43]

Since then, Séléka – a loose coalition of factions and armed groups, including the Union of Democratic Forces for Unity, the Convention of Patriots for Justice and Peace, and the Patriotic Convention for Saving the Country, amongst others – has been one of the most commonly cited groups in statements about ivory as a conflict resource.[44] The US Global

[41] Hannah Osborne, 'Elephant Herd Massacred in Central African Republic National Park', *International Business Times*, 10 May 2013.

[42] *The Guardian*, 'Central African Republic Humanitarian Crisis Deepens Following Coup', 26 March 2013.

[43] UN News Centre, 'UN Envoy Calls on International Community to Engage More with Central African Republic', 11 January 2013; WWF, 'Poachers Storm "Village of Elephants"', 7 May 2013.

[44] Warren Manger, 'Ivory Poaching's Direct Links to the World's Most Evil Terrorists, Warlords and Dictators is Exposed', *The Mirror*, 18 September 2015.

Anti-Poaching Act, passed in June 2015, denounced Séléka for both supporting and drawing funding from wildlife trafficking.[45] Séléka also featured in journalist Bryan Christy's reporting for *National Geographic*, accused of supporting ivory poaching and trafficking in CAR.[46] Other analysts have taken this further, describing 'blood ivory' as Séléka's 'savings account' and attributing its 2013 seizure of power directly to funds gained from ivory.[47] In 2015, UN Security Council Resolution 2217 explicitly stated that 'illicit trade, exploitation and smuggling of natural resources including … wildlife poaching and trafficking continues to threaten the peace and stability of the CAR'.[48] It did so noting 'that poaching and trafficking of wildlife are among the factors that fuel the crisis in the CAR'.[49]

Séléka emerged in northeastern CAR in 2012 in the context of long-term government abandonment of the Muslim north and the apparent exertion of growing influence and provision of support to armed groups in the region by neighbouring Chad and Sudan.[50] Séléka's ousting of longstanding President François Bozizé in 2013 marked a dramatic reversal of CAR's traditionally Christian-dominated political landscape; for the first time, a force stemming from the country's northern and eastern Muslim population occupied the seat of power.[51] As the country was plunged into crisis, the instrumentalisation of religion exacerbated an upsurge in collective violence and intercommunal reprisals. The result was a deepening of societal fractures, in effect dividing the country along religious lines.[52]

In early 2014, the Séléka regime led by Michel Djotodia was forced under international pressure to resign, making way for a transitional government and the organisation of democratic elections. Since then, the situation has grown calmer, but not without the conflict claiming around

---

45 Foreign Affairs Committee, 'H.R. 2494, Eliminate, Neutralize, and Disrupt Wildlife Trafficking Act', 25 June 2015, <https://foreignaffairs.house.gov/legislation/h-r-2494-global-anti-poaching-act/>, accessed 26 September 2016.

46 Bryan Christy, 'How Killing Elephants Finances Terror in Africa', *National Geographic*, 12 August 2015.

47 Todd Maxwell Pelfrey, 'Africa: Poachers and Blood Ivory', presentation to the Quest Club, 15 January 2016.

48 *Ibid*.

49 UN Security Council, 'Resolution 2217 (2015), Adopted by the Security Council at its 7434th meeting, on 28 April 2015', S/RES/2217 (2015), preamble.

50 International Crisis Group (ICG), 'Central African Republic: The Roots of Violence', Africa Report No. 230, 21 September 2015.

51 *The Economist*, 'No One is in Charge of the Central African Republic', 8 January 2016.

52 ICG, 'Central African Republic'.

6,000 lives and displacing a quarter of CAR's population.[53] This national collapse played out despite the efforts of an African-led International Support Mission to the Central African Republic (MISCA) – later the UN Multidimensional Integrated Stabilization Mission in CAR (MINUSCA). MISCA was authorised in December 2013 to work alongside French troops deployed under Operation *Sangaris* to stabilise the country, transferring its authority to MINUSCA in September 2014.[54]

The impact of the conflict on CAR's abundant wildlife has been substantial. Dzanga Sangha is one of the areas to have felt the effects most strongly – the slaughter at Dzanga Bai was not an isolated incident.[55] The park holds many riches: it is one of the last bastions for forest elephants, the last multi-ton ivory source in CAR,[56] and an abundant source of diamonds and gold, all located within pristine primary forest. The key question concerns the extent to which Séléka targeted this park and others for the bounties they offer, and the extent to which ivory and other resources served as fuel for the conflict as it played out.

CAR is landlocked, surrounded by six neighbours, of which four – DRC, South Sudan, Sudan and Chad – have witnessed repeated instances of armed conflict. Conflict dynamics here have in turn long been connected to the region's abundance of natural resources. Dzanga Sangha forms a core part of this environment: it is one of a series of adjacent transnational parks, sharing borders with Lobéké National Park in Cameroon and Nouabalé-Ndoki National Park in the Republic of Congo. Together, these parks comprise the broader Sangha River Tri-National Protected Area, covering almost 7,770 square kilometres and labelled a UNESCO World Heritage Site in July 2012.[57]

Recent research shows that the Protected Area was highly prized in the power struggle that engulfed CAR in 2013.[58] Fears that a 'perfect

---

[53] Council on Foreign Relations, 'Violence in the Central African Republic', 11 April 2016.

[54] MISCA was itself preceded by a strengthened UN Integrated Peacebuilding Office in the Central African Republic (BINUCA). See UN, 'MINUSCA Background', <http://www.un.org/en/peacekeeping/missions/minusca/background.shtml>, accessed 6 August 2016.

[55] WWF, 'Field Reports Indicate Slaughter of Elephants, Conservation Staff Evacuated', 25 April 2013.

[56] Samuel K Wasser et al., 'Genetic Assignment of Large Seizures of Elephant Ivory Reveals Africa's Major Poaching Hotspots', *Science* (Vol. 349, No. 6243, 2015).

[57] Dzanga Sangha National Park, 'The Sangha River Tri-National Protected Area (STN)', <http://www.dzanga-sangha.org/node/309>, accessed 15 May 2016; *Congo-site*, 'Le site tri-national de la Sangha inscrit au patrimoine mondial de l'UNESCO', 5 July 2012.

[58] Terrence Fuh Neba and David Greer, 'Update: Conflict in the Central African Republic', *Gorilla Journal* (November 2014), <http://www.berggorilla.org/en/

storm' of war and anarchy was crashing into fragile wildlife populations seemed confirmed when Séléka forces arrived in Bayanga, Dzanga Sangha's main town, ransacking and looting Dzanga Sangha/WWF headquarters in April 2013.[59] This and other repeated instances of violence and looting were followed in May by the Dzanga Bai elephant massacre, a methodical attack by experienced Sudanese poachers armed with automatic rifles. Indicative of the value of Dzanga Sangha to Séléka in its struggle to consolidate power, a company of Séléka troops was stationed in Bayanga in April 2013. The town witnessed regular visits by support troops from a larger base in the town of Nola, 120 km to the north.[60] Speaking to the complexity of the conflict dynamics at play, conservationists and researchers Terence Fuh Neba and David Greer suggest that at least three different splinter Séléka groups, reporting to different leaders, visited Dzanga Sangha over an eleven-month period, during which the lootings and elephant killings took place.[61]

Ivory – alongside Dzanga Sangha's abundance of other lootable natural resources – would undoubtedly have been viewed as an important commodity for a new Séléka government seeking to establish control over an unstable country – and needing to pay off allied forces from Chad or Sudan, which had provided manpower and firepower. Facing violent reprisals by Anti-Balaka militias – and with the prospect of sectarian civil war,[62] the challenge of maintaining internal cohesion,[63] and international isolation – Séléka's need for ready access to funding and resources is clear. In line with this, evidence suggests a prioritisation of natural resource acquisition: a Séléka commander was reportedly stationed at Bayanga, for example, with responsibility for protecting Chinese diamond prospectors.[64] Later investigations have suggested his complicity in the Dzanga Bai elephant massacre. The Sudanese poachers responsible were reportedly in possession of a mission order from both Séléka's newly established Ministry of Defence and Ministry of Water and Forests,

---

gorillas/threats-protection/threats/articles-threats/update-conflict-in-the-central-african-republic-1/>, accessed 22 June 2016.

[59] Since its opening in the late 1980s, Dzanga Sangha has been supported by the WWF, headquartered in the village of Bayanga. Author interview with Terence Fuh Neba, WWF, Dzanga Sangha, November 2014. See also Neba and Greer, 'Update: Conflict in the Central African Republic'.

[60] Neba and Greer, 'Update: Conflict in the Central African Republic'.

[61] *Ibid.*

[62] David Smith, 'Christian Militias Take Bloody Revenge on Muslims in Central African Republic', *The Guardian*, 10 March 2014.

[63] Jacey Fortin, 'Deadly Conflict Spirals Out of Control in Central African Republic as Foreign Troops Deploy', *International Business Times*, 12 October 2013.

[64] Laurel Neme, 'Chaos and Confusion Following Elephant Poaching in a Central African World Heritage Site', *National Geographic*, 13 May 2013.

authorising their presence in the park. They were reportedly granted entry to the park as payment for mercenary services rendered, in spite of protests by park officials to the local Séléka commander.[65] However, it must be noted that this evidence remains partial, with the existence of a mission order never proven.

Further research by the UN Panel of Experts on CAR, the International Peace Information Service and US-based NGO the Enough Project points to evidence that Séléka had provided Sudanese poachers with weapons and ammunition to poach on its behalf – and, beyond this, had been involved in poaching directly.[66] These organisations' research points to Séléka combatants killing twelve elephants for their tusks in February 2013 near the Ecofaune ranger post in Sangba.[67] Beyond this, there have been reports of major stockpile thefts by Séléka forces; upon taking control of Bangui in March 2013, the group is reported to have pillaged a stockpile of more than 100 seized tusks and weapons stored in the Ministry of Water and Forests.[68] Meanwhile, primary research by one of the authors indicates that Séléka was not the only conflict party involved. This research reveals participation by victorious anti-Balaka forces allied to criminal networks not only in ivory trafficking, but also in trafficking in diamonds and timber following Séléka's withdrawal from Bangui – with these groups possessing the firepower to hold back MINUSCA troops at border crossings for long enough to allow these activities to take place.[69]

This evidence is far from comprehensive or complete, but suggests that the narrative on a link between ivory and conflict actors has some basis in reality, at least in the case of CAR. However, it requires a higher standard of proof to confirm the role of ivory as a *funder* of the conflict, as has been asserted by some politicians and the media. Such proof does not yet exist in this case – an issue that also affects case studies of ivory as a funder of terrorism examined in Chapter III. In the case of CAR, the

---

[65] Peter Canby, 'Elephant Watch', *New Yorker*, 11 May 2015; Yannick Weyns et al., 'Mapping Conflict Motives in the Central African Republic', International Peace Information Service, November 2014, p. 41; UN Security Council, 'Report of the Panel of Experts on the Central African Republic Established Pursuant to Security Council Resolution 2127 (2013)', S/2014/452, 1 July 2014, p. 20.

[66] UN Security Council, 'Report of the Panel of Experts on the Central African Republic Established Pursuant to Security Council Resolution 2127 (2013)', p. 19.

[67] *Ibid.*; Kasper Agger, 'Behind the Headlines: Drivers of Violence in the Central African Republic', Enough Project, May 2014.

[68] UN Security Council, 'Report of the Panel of Experts on the Central African Republic Established Pursuant to Security Council Resolution 2127 (2013)', p. 19.

[69] Author interview with Congolese lieutenant, MINUSCA, Nola, CAR, December 2014.

most that can reliably be asserted is an *intersection* between ivory and conflict during 2013–14.

Even if public narratives can be corrected to an intersection between ivory and conflict, issues arise in the way in which incomplete evidence is translated into often generalised statements. Incomplete evidence in specific locations is commonly translated into blanket statements presenting ivory – and indeed wildlife more broadly – as having destabilising impacts wherever elephants and conflict coexist.[70] The existence of select evidence, for example in CAR, however, does not imply that poaching and trafficking of ivory by conflict parties *always* takes place in biodiversity-rich areas. Instead, it is crucial that assertions of ivory as a conflict resource are contextualised, accompanied by specific and nuanced reference to particular cases where evidence exists.

Even where reference is made to specific cases, such as CAR, there is a tendency to oversimplify. Statements aiming to raise the profile of ivory as a conflict resource have at times treated the commodity in isolation from other sources of finance on which armed groups such as Séléka can draw,[71] thereby ignoring these groups' wider financing strategies. Such a misrepresentation of the picture on the ground can serve to distort responses. In the case of CAR, the potentially relatively limited proportion of rebel finance derived from ivory compared with other resources is often unacknowledged.

Indeed, gold and diamonds are also known to have played a role in CAR's conflict, with no evidence to suggest that ivory was of greater significance than these and other resources.[72] To the contrary, as Séléka's tenure in Bangui progressed, research by the authors suggests that Séléka's harvesting activities increasingly focused on mineral extraction on Dzanga Sangha's fringes, with minerals accessed increasingly easily relative to shrinking elephant populations.[73] There is also some evidence to suggest that one of the Séléka commanders in Bayanga gradually came to moderate the activities of Sudanese poachers in the area. After evacuating its staff, in August 2013 WWF employed Maisha Consulting, an environmental security firm, to establish a presence in the park and make contact with Séléka. Over several deployments, the team eventually crafted an agreement to spare wildlife, allowing patrols to resume without

---

[70] See, for example, Schiffman, 'Ivory Poaching Funds Most War and Terrorism in Africa'.
[71] Christy, 'How Killing Elephants Finances Terror in Africa'.
[72] UN Security Council Resolution 2217.
[73] WWF–Dzanga Sangha Protected Areas After-Action Anti-Poaching Reports, January 2015.

challenging or sanctioning Séléka's authority.[74] In 2014 and 2015, one of the authors worked to consolidate Maisha Consulting's efforts on intelligence gathering and law enforcement after the team's departure. With Séléka's 2014 retreat from southwest CAR, and thus from Dzanga Sangha, it became clear that ivory had ceased to be as reliable a source of income for the group as it might have been previously. Meanwhile, there is evidence to suggest that crime syndicates, some supported by national officials, took over poaching and mining. This has produced perhaps a greater long-term threat to wildlife as the conflict subsided into low-intensity warfare, out of sight and mind of the international community.[75]

This points to another way in which oversimplification of the ivory–conflict link risks obscuring key parts of the picture. Crucially, there is a tendency to portray the conflict actor in question, in this case Séléka, as acting alone in exploiting ivory, and to neglect other organisations involved. This relates to the fact that conflict actors are likely to attract most attention from security professionals and policymakers. However, a focus on insurgent groups to the exclusion of other participating groups – including those without a direct interest in the conflict – risks distorting a more complex reality.

Supporting this, in CAR, research by one of the authors in the form of extended periods of fieldwork in and around Dzanga Sangha suggests that established Central African poaching gangs and criminal networks have long constituted – and continue to constitute – the main threats to Dzanga Sangha's wildlife, sourcing proportionally far greater quantities of ivory through regular poaching operations facilitated by corrupt officials.[76] Under Séléka occupation, elephant losses rose only slightly,[77] while the retreat of Séléka forces from Bangui, and with it the group's loss of direct access to Dzanga Sangha, did not significantly improve poaching levels in the park.[78] Although there have been no further elephant massacres, the

[74] Author interview with chief executive officer of Maisha Consulting, Bayanga, CAR, September 2014; Varun Vira and Thomas Ewing, 'Ivory's Curse: The Militarization and Professionalization of Poaching in Africa', C4ADS and Born Free USA, April 2014, pp. 31–32; Canby, 'Elephant Watch'; Hilo Glazer, 'Heart of Darkness: Israeli Expedition Hunts Elephant Killers in Africa', *Haaretz*, 9 November 2013.

[75] Author interview with Central African army sergeant complicit in trafficking, corroborated by author interviews with Dzanga Sangha conservation warden and ranger team leaders, Bayanga, CAR, January 2015.

[76] WWF–Dzanga Sangha Protected Areas After-Action Anti-Poaching Patrol Reports and Dzanga Sangha Protected Areas authority investigations, March 2015.

[77] Vira and Ewing, 'Ivory's Curse', pp. 31–32.

[78] *Ibid.*, pp. 31–32; UN Security Council, 'Report of the Panel of Experts on the Central African Republic Established Pursuant to Security Council Resolution 2127 (2013)', p. 19.

level of killing has remained high. Between mid-2014 and mid-2015, there were an estimated two to four poaching incidents a month (excluding those that inevitably go unreported and undetected).[79] As such, it is clear that the threat to Dzanga Sangha is posed by a much broader range of groups and individuals whose specific interests range from subsistence hunting to opportunistic poaching and commercial, organised cross-border ivory harvesting. It is also worth noting, however, that these actors' operations can and do intersect. Both criminal and conflict actors appear at times to work in collaboration as interests dictate, feeding into a complex reality in which numerous forces coordinate ivory poaching and trafficking.[80]

Supporting this analysis of broader-based participation at a global level is wider research by a range of organisations highlighting the far more significant role in the global illegal ivory trade played by non-insurgent poachers. This research also indicates the relatively limited extent to which conflict parties' ability to engage in ivory trade is likely, alone, to fuel ongoing conflict. A 2013 report by the UN Environment Programme (UNEP) assessed the likely proportional role played by conflict actors in the ivory trade and, conversely, the value of ivory to conflict actors. It did so noting that, unlike timber or minerals, 'the value of ivory is not enough alone to fund a war'.[81] A joint UNEP and INTERPOL report in 2014 sought to put this into further context. It calculated that the number of projected poached elephants within striking range of militant groups was sufficiently limited to suggest that the entire value of the ivory trade to sub-Saharan rebel or insurgent groups would be unlikely to exceed $4–12.2 million per year.[82]

While such figures are difficult to calculate accurately, the point is fundamental: these groups are neither likely to be able to profit significantly and exclusively from ivory, nor are they major players in an ivory market of many times this magnitude. Rather, in locations such as CAR, it is more likely the intersection of the broader conflict dynamics they sustain with the much larger-scale operations of established criminal

---

[79] Internal WWF/Dzanga Sangha Protected Areas After-Action Anti-Poaching Patrol Reports, May 2015, and law enforcement monitoring tools (SMART, GIS and local intelligence gathering).

[80] Author interview with ranger team leader patrolling in northern Dzanga Sangha Protected Areas, Nola, Bayanga, CAR, April 2015. This ranger team leader reported Anti-Balaka mining of illegal diamonds while employing poachers, and local army units poaching ivory and selling elephant meat.

[81] Nellemann et al. (eds), *Elephants in the Dust*, p. 58.

[82] Christian Nellemann et al. (eds), *The Environmental Crime Crisis – Threats to Sustainable Development from Illegal Exploitation and Trade in Wildlife and Forest Resources* (Nairobi and Arendal: UNEP and Grid-Arendal, 2014), p. 8.

traffickers that threaten the survival of elephant populations. Adding to previous research, the relative importance of criminal rather than conflict actors was assessed by the UN Office on Drugs and Crime (UNODC) in its 2016 report by considering the elephant numbers in Africa upon which each set of actors could feasibly draw. Drawing on data relating to eleven countries with insurgencies and 43 countries at peace, UNODC concluded that elephants in countries with insurgency number only 20,405, while elephants in countries at peace number 453,392.[83] This suggests far greater opportunities for criminal rather than conflict actors to profit from ivory poaching and trafficking in the future.

Policy Implications

Although CAR is just one case study (Chapter III examines the main cases cited to demonstrate an ivory–terrorism link), it suggests that greater nuance and more careful consideration are required in prevailing narratives on ivory as a conflict resource. Such nuance is also key to the design of effective measures to address poaching and ivory trafficking on the ground. Where a discourse linking conflict, poaching and ivory trafficking emerges, the tendency is to embrace militarised responses. At times, these are characterised by a targeted dovetailing of anti-poaching and counterinsurgency strategies, albeit with responses tailored to the differences inherent to a conflict zone and a tourist park.[84]

Indeed, it is clear that conservation cannot remain a peaceful or unarmed endeavour as long as the operational context is one of civil conflict, overtly hostile to both humans and wildlife. It would be both environmentally destructive and morally irresponsible to force practitioners on the ground to counter deadly threats in a conflict zone unarmed. In CAR, for example, the complexities of contemporary poaching trends, compounded by a national and violent political and security crisis, have forced practices in parks such as Dzanga Sangha to evolve, stepping up to a more militarised threat.

Efforts to defund conflict via anti-poaching are, however, criticised by some observers, who cite the other incentives potentially available – offering

[83] See UNODC, *World Wildlife Crime Report: Trafficking in Protected Species, 2016* (New York, NY: UN, 2016), p. 44, Figure 4. The numbers presented are calculated on the basis of data from the IUCN Species Survival Commission's African Elephant Specialist Group, covering both 'definite' and 'probable' elephant numbers. In this calculation, it is noted that countries with insurgencies include those affected by Boko Haram (Cameroon, Chad, Niger and Nigeria), the LRA (CAR, DRC and Sudan), civil war (South Sudan, CAR and Somalia), and the various insurgent groups active in DRC, Ethiopia and Burundi.

[84] Somerville, *Ivory*, pp. 303–04.

source country governments, for example, greater access to Western funding, as well as logistical and surveillance support in the fight against domestic or regional opponents. Critics also point to their potential to deflect attention from the corruption, patronage networks and weak judicial systems that allow the broader trade to flourish.[85] Such approaches could also, they observe, potentially allow Western states a softer pitch, whether to domestic or international audiences, for the use of aggressive tactics against destabilising actors. (It must be noted, however, that evidence to underpin such criticism does not yet exist.[86])

The 2010s have seen the West provide greater financial support for anti-poaching activity. For example, the US, the UK and France have increased their support to enforcement operations in countries such as Kenya, Chad and Gabon,[87] including the deployment of military advisers to train anti-poaching units.[88] As Jasper Humphreys and M L R Smith point out, in many of these countries, 'The intensification of the counter-poaching strategy is clearly part of a trend that has witnessed the increasing militarization of wildlife management', while 'the physical manifestation of this approach also bears resemblance to some notable developments in … a policy of enhanced confrontation with the poachers'.[89] The evolution of anti-poaching strategies, and a drift towards the coordination of counterinsurgency and wildlife law enforcement in conflict zones such as CAR, is worth examining in this regard.

First, as evidence of an intersection between armed groups such as Séléka and ivory poaching and trafficking has emerged, a series of resolutions and practical measures have been approved and implemented by the international community. The December 2013 embargo on arms, military equipment and training imposed on CAR under UN Security Council Resolution 2127 was notable for its exemption of 'Supplies of small arms and other related equipment intended solely for use in international patrols providing security in the Sangha River Tri-National Protected Area to defend against poaching, [and the] smuggling of ivory and arms'.[90] This was the first time a UN Security Council Resolution had

85 *Ibid.*

86 *Ibid.*

87 Ministry of Defence, 'British Forces Support Gabon's Fight against Elephant Poachers', 28 April 2016, <https://www.gov.uk/government/news/british-forces-support-gabons-fight-against-elephant-poachers>, accessed 14 July 2016.

88 Somerville, *Ivory*, p. 258.

89 Jasper Humphreys and M L R Smith, 'The "Rhinofication" of South African Security', *International Affairs* (Vol. 90, No. 4, 2014).

90 UN Security Council, 'Resolution 2127 (2013) Adopted by the Security Council at its 7072nd meeting, on 5 December 2013', S/RES/2127 (2013), 5 December 2013, para. 54 (d).

specified an exception to an arms embargo in relation to a national park – recognition of Dzanga Sangha's value both to global biodiversity and to conflict actors in CAR.

At the same time, Resolution 2127 formally asserted the existence of a link between illegal exploitation of ivory and the reinforcement of armed groups in CAR. It acknowledged that 'poaching and trafficking of wildlife are among the factors that fuel the crisis in the CAR', expressing its 'condemnation of the devastation of natural heritage' through these processes.[91] The resolution went further in reiterating 'the importance of bringing an end to these illegal activities, including by applying the necessary pressure on the armed groups, traffickers and all other actors involved'.[92] In 2015, Resolution 2217 called on 'the CAR, its neighbouring States and other member States of the International Conference on the Great Lakes Region … to cooperate at the regional level to investigate and combat regional criminal networks and armed groups involved in … wildlife poaching and trafficking' in CAR.[93] In doing so, the UN Security Council in effect formally acknowledged illegal natural resource exploitation in CAR – including ivory poaching and trafficking – as a threat to peace and security.

Under Chapter VII of the UN Charter, this characterisation of ivory poaching and trafficking as a threat to peace and security opens the door for potentially coercive countermeasures, including the use of peacekeeping forces to fight armed groups involved in such activity. In March and June 2015, MINUSCA troops worked in partnership with the Dzanga Sangha administration, with WWF technical support, to perform anti-poaching operations, contributing to patrols, seizures and arrests.[94] Taking this further, bodies such as the International Crisis Group have called on the UN, specialised organisations, regional states and the CAR government to create a dedicated cell within MINUSCA to counter ivory trafficking, as well as diamond and gold smuggling, citing their apparent role in funding conflict.[95]

At the domestic level, CAR rangers are already mandated by the Ministry of Water and Forests to carry and use 'weapons of war',[96] with wildlife law enforcement being de jure paramilitary (unlike in countries

---

91 *Ibid.*, preamble.

92 *Ibid.*, para. 16.

93 UN Security Council Resolution 2217, para. 38.

94 Author interviews with Dzanga Sangha Protected Areas ranger in charge of operations and law enforcement, Bayanga, CAR, June 2015.

95 ICG, 'The Central African Crisis: From Predation to Stabilisation', Africa Report No. 219, 17 June 2014, p. 4.

96 This term describes weapons and ammunition classified as war material, including AK-47 assault rifles and belt-fed machine guns (7.62 mm), MAS model 36 bolt-action rifles (7.5 mm), pistols and automatic sub-machine guns (9 mm).

such as Cameroon).[97] The outbreak of conflict saw this militarised mandate stepped up. For WWF and Dzanga Sangha, enforcing wildlife law and denying access to wildlife resources at the 'point of the crime' within a conflict environment has involved providing rangers with training in infantry tactics, as well as investing in self-defence and advanced first-aid training. Dzanga Sangha's enforcement contingent comprises 80 rangers and trackers responsible for ecological monitoring and enforcement of laws regulating fauna, mining and logging inside protected areas. However, the level of threats faced has left the rangers overstretched – despite patrolling for a total of 21 days a month. This means that they are currently unable to provide optimal surveillance and coverage, due to low numbers and lack of equipment. More resources and technological force multipliers are therefore required to fulfil the missions they are charged with.

The approach adopted in Dzanga Sangha was formally documented in the 2015 Dzanga Sangha Protected Areas Anti-Poaching Strategy (albeit drafted in a post-conflict context). The strategy was designed to respond to an array of interwoven pressures set against a background of ongoing instability and insecurity – from natural habitat destruction to poaching, risk of violent conflict, poverty and corruption.[98] The strategy attempts to address these threats simultaneously through a multidisciplinary enforcement approach that incorporates both hard and soft power elements. Key to the latter are efforts to support local communities as part of an inclusive strategy, creating stewards of wildlife and natural resources as part of medium- and long-term solutions. This combination of approaches recalls measures found in contemporary counterinsurgency doctrines. Applied to wildlife law enforcement, this is the foundation of the concept of 'counterpoaching', which seeks to serve both conservation and peacemaking efforts by defunding conflict actors and enhancing stability.

Counterpoaching, employed where conservation is faced with militarised threats, can serve to preserve wildlife and counter illegal natural resource extraction by enhancing law enforcement and combating small arms proliferation on a small scale. However, the effectiveness of counterpoaching in defunding conflict will depend on the extent to which conflict parties rely on ivory poaching and trafficking as a source of funding. The success of these measures will also depend on the extent to

97 Cameroonian rangers do not carry firearms but are reinforced by the army when judged necessary, creating significant gaps when on-the-spot coercion is needed for protection and law enforcement.

98 Given the circumstances facing Dzanga Sangha, the 2015 strategy was introduced to update the 2012 strategy, covering necessary adaptations to wildlife law enforcement.

which other actors are also engaged in ivory poaching and trafficking, whether for criminal profit-making or to meet subsistence needs. Where these latter actors play a significant role in ivory poaching and trafficking, counterpoaching operations will not necessarily have a direct or significant impact on the activities of conflict parties. The result is limited influence over the economics of conflict in these locations.

Furthermore, in most contexts, counterpoaching cannot put an end to, or prevent a resurgence of, conflict – especially where, as in CAR, root causes lie in much wider socioeconomic, political and religious dynamics and grievances.[99] These grievances can be addressed only through a political process and through long-term structural, institutional and socioeconomic reform rooted in inclusive dialogue. A heavily militarised approach to countering ivory poaching and trafficking – inspired in part by the narrative that conflict parties are major drivers and beneficiaries of these activities – brings its own security implications and dynamics. These dynamics can intertwine in unpredictable ways with existing political and economic grievances.

Such considerations are also crucial to any future movement towards formal classification of ivory as a conflict resource. In 2015, *National Geographic* published a letter to the UN General Assembly arguing that the time had come to formally recognise 'conflict ivory'.[100] The letter lamented the fact that only conflict diamonds had received recognition by the UN General Assembly – under Resolution 55/56 of December 2000 – and that the passage of a formal resolution on conflict ivory 'would help elevate on international agendas the crisis elephants face by linking it to human violence'.[101] While this may be true, it is essential to consider the impact of reiterating an ivory–insurgency connection given the tendency towards oversimplified narratives, and the resultant risk of distorted policies. It must be remembered that conflict ivory is unlikely to form a major part of the illegal ivory trade relative to the more significant roles played by subsistence hunting, opportunistic poaching and organised criminal harvesting. As such, while limiting ivory harvesting by any group (violent or otherwise) will be beneficial to wider conservation and natural resource management efforts, it is crucial that further debates on ivory and conflict are kept in the appropriate perspective.

---

[99] ICG, 'Central African Republic'.

[100] Katarzyna Nowak, 'Letter to the United Nations General Assembly: It is Time to Formally Recognize Conflict Ivory', A Voice for Elephants blog, *National Geographic*, 21 September 2015.

[101] *Ibid.*

III. POACHING, WILDLIFE TRAFFICKING AND TERRORISM

CATHY HAENLEIN, THOMAS MAGUIRE AND KEITH SOMERVILLE

The possible link between poaching, wildlife trafficking and terrorism is a frequent feature of public narratives.[1] These narratives often emphasise the implications of this link for transnational security as well as domestic conflict (the latter is examined in Chapter II). Indeed, the assertion that terrorist groups in African range states are major drivers of the current poaching crisis has rapidly become a common feature of debates on the threat posed by poaching and wildlife trafficking.[2] As the trade has grown in scale, and as concern about its security dimensions has mounted, the 'poaching–wildlife trafficking–terrorism nexus' has emerged as an ever more potent narrative.[3]

Deftly tapping into two hot-button issues, the image of terrorists decimating iconic land mammals elicits strong reactions. Described, for example, by US film director Kathryn Bigelow as 'the diabolical

---

[1] Aggrey Mutambo, 'US State Department Links Poaching to Terrorism', *Daily Nation*, 15 November 2013; Catrina Stewart, 'Illegal Ivory Trade Funds Al-Shabaab's Terrorist Attacks', *The Independent*, 5 October 2013; Monica Medina, 'The White Gold of Jihad', *New York Times*, 30 September 2013.

[2] Carla Sterley, 'Elephants and Rhinos Fund Terror Networks: Illegal Poaching in Sub-Saharan Africa Funds Islamic Fundamentalism', Consultancy Africa Intelligence, 9 September 2014; Liana Sun Wyler and Pervaze A Sheikh, 'International Illegal Trade in Wildlife: Threats and U.S. Policy', Congressional Research Service Report for Congress, 22 August 2008, Congressional Research Service, RL34395, 2008, pp. 11, 21; Mutambo, 'US State Department Links Poaching to Terrorism'.

[3] Tom Maguire and Cathy Haenlein, 'An Illusion of Complicity: Terrorism and the Illegal Ivory Trade in East Africa', *RUSI Occasional Papers* (September 2015).

intersection of two problems … of great concern – species extinction and global terrorism', a poaching–terrorism link naturally whips up human sentiment wherever the possibility is raised.[4] This chapter examines the evidence underpinning claims of widespread participation by terrorist groups in the illegal ivory trade. Specifically, it considers the assertions that Al-Shabaab, the Janjaweed and the Lord's Resistance Army (LRA) – the three most commonly cited groups – have become major beneficiaries.

The Tenuous Tusk–Terror Tie

The argument that ivory plays a key role in financing terrorism has become embedded in public discourse in both Western and African states.[5] The argument first began to circulate in the early 2010s, alongside broader discussions about conflict ivory (see Chapter II). Both narratives gained traction as part of two wider discourses then occupying policy, academic and think tank communities. The first concerned growing fears over the national, regional and international security implications of an expanding wildlife trafficking crisis – despite a lack of clarity on what precisely those implications were.[6] The second concerned growing fears in Western countries about regional conflicts in Africa becoming breeding grounds for insurgencies that could ally themselves with groups such as Al-Qa'ida – seen as a permanent threat to Western interests – and that these movements could fund themselves through criminal activities, in line with post-9/11 'crime–terror nexus' theories.[7]

In this context, the temptation to link poaching and trafficking, particularly of ivory, with terrorism is clearly great. The prospect is emotive, drawing on the archetypes surrounding 'poachers' and 'poaching' on the one hand – especially of much-loved mammals such as elephants and rhinos – and 'terrorists' and 'terrorism' on the other.

[4] See Nolan Feeney, 'Premiere: Watch Kathryn Bigelow's Short Film about Elephant Poaching, Last Days', *Time*, 4 December 2014.

[5] Rosaleen Duffy, 'Al-Shabaab and Ivory (1)', Marjan Centre for the Study of War and the Non-Human Sphere, 26 September 2015.

[6] See Johan Bergenas and Ariella Knight, 'Green Terror: Environmental Crime and Illicit Financing', *SAIS Review of International Affairs* (Vol. 35, No. 1, 2015); International Fund for Animal Welfare (IFAW), 'Criminal Nature: The Global Security Implications of the Illegal Wildlife Trade', June 2013.

[7] See Tamara Makarenko, 'The Crime–Terror Continuum: Tracing the Interplay Between Transnational Organised Crime and Terrorism', *Global Crime* (Vol. 6, No. 1, 2004); Chris Dishman, 'The Leaderless Nexus: When Crime and Terror Converge', *Studies in Conflict and Terrorism* (Vol. 28, No. 3, 2005); John T Picarelli, 'The Turbulent Nexus Of Transnational Organised Crime And Terrorism: A Theory of Malevolent International Relations', *Global Crime* (Vol. 7, No. 1, 2006).

This imagery has appeared to act as a pull for media outlets looking to sell newspapers, conservation campaigners seeking donations, researchers pursuing prominent profiles and politicians seeking support for legislation. Many have embraced the narrative linking ivory poaching and trafficking with terrorism and, further, appeared keen actively to perpetuate it.

A number of organisations designated as terrorist are also said to have gained substantial funding from ivory trafficking. The most frequently cited are Al-Shabaab, operating from its base in Somalia across the broader Horn of Africa; the LRA, operating in northeastern Democratic Republic of the Congo (DRC), southern Central African Republic (CAR) and southwestern South Sudan; and the Janjaweed, operating from Darfur across Central Africa.[8] Demonstrating a longstanding confusion in the West over how to conceptualise conflict and organised violence in Africa, the labelling of these groups as terrorist organisations is inconsistent. Al-Shabaab is the only group designated a 'Foreign Terrorist Organization' by the US State Department. The Janjaweed and LRA are nonetheless frequently labelled as terrorist groups by the media, research institutes and policymakers.[9]

Of course, adjudicating on whether a group is a terrorist group, and what constitutes 'terrorism', are fluid and often deeply politicised debates fraught with complexities.[10] Most definitions – such as that proffered by Alex P Schmid – require terrorist groups, and acts of terror, to be driven predominantly by political motivations.[11] Generally, terrorist organisations are described, as by the US Department of Defense, as those that exist to threaten or engage in violence to 'coerce or intimidate governments or

---

[8] Some news sources have (much less frequently) also cited Boko Haram in northern Nigeria and Daesh (also known as the Islamic State of Iraq and Syria, ISIS) as beneficiaries. See, for example, Brandon Keim and Emma Howard, 'African "Blood Ivory" Destroyed in New York to Signal Crackdown on Illegal Trade', *The Guardian*, 19 June 2015.

[9] US Department of State, Bureau of Counterterrorism, 'Foreign Terrorist Organizations', <http://www.state.gov/j/ct/rls/other/des/123085.htm>, accessed 16 April 2016. Both the Janjaweed and LRA, for example, appear on the Terrorism Research and Analysis Consortium's (TRAC) database, <http://www.trackingterrorism.org/>, and in well-regarded publications such as Gus Martin, *Understanding Terrorism: Challenges, Perspectives, and Issues*, 4th edition (London: Sage, 2013), pp. 277–78.

[10] Jacqueline Hodgson and Victor Tadros, 'The Impossibility of Defining Terrorism', *New Criminal Law Review* (Vol. 16, No. 3, 2013); Leonard Weinberg, Ami Pedahzur and Sivan Hirsch-Hoefler, 'The Challenges of Conceptualizing Terrorism', *Terrorism and Political Violence* (Vol. 16, No. 4, 2004).

[11] Alex P Schmid, 'Terrorism as Psychological Warfare', *Democracy and Security* (Vol. 1, No. 2, 2005).

societies in the pursuit of goals that are generally political, religious, or ideological'.[12] Yet a lack of clarity remains about the terrorist credentials of a range of organisations: terrorism databases such as the Terrorism Research and Analysis Consortium's database, the University of Maryland's state-sponsored Study of Terrorism and Responses to Terrorism Global Terrorism Database and the US National Counterterrorism Center's Counterterrorism Guide all differ in their analysis of particular organisations. At the same time, reflecting this confusion, the rise of the ivory–terrorism narrative has seen Al-Shabaab, the Janjaweed and the LRA lumped together under a single 'terrorist' label, despite these groups' very different histories, aims and motivations.

Al-Shabaab and Ivory in East Africa

Al-Shabaab – the Al-Qa'ida-affiliated Somali jihadi Islamist organisation – has featured perhaps the most strongly in claims of participation in ivory poaching and trafficking. Undoubtedly, such attention is linked to its status as the only one of these three groups that can be considered as posing any threat to the West. The group emerged as the most militant faction of the Islamic Courts Union in 2006, growing rapidly into a well-organised force able to mount sophisticated attacks and build governance structures in the chaos left by the collapse of the Somali state in the early 1990s.[13] In light of its Al-Qa'ida affiliation, articulated ideological and political goals, and fear-inspiring violent tactics, few in the West contest its terrorist credentials. As it has evolved, it has also expanded – particularly since 2011 – beyond its traditional base into Kenya. The result has been an ability to recruit, fundraise and launch devastating attacks on the Kenyan state, which it seeks to destroy in order to free Kenyan Muslims from perceived oppression.[14]

The group's growing influence in Kenya has also prompted concern over its access to elephants, Somalia's own elephant populations having long since disappeared. This has in turn led to widely repeated assertions that Al-Shabaab has come to profit significantly from illegal ivory. These assertions rest on two claims. The first is that the organisation engages directly in poaching Kenyan elephants. The second is that Al-Shabaab

[12] See Joint Chiefs of Staff, Department of Defense, *Department of Defense Dictionary of Military and Associated Terms* (Washington, DC: Department of Defense, 2008).

[13] Stig Jarle Hansen, *Al-Shabaab in Somalia: The History and Ideology of a Militant Islamist Group: 2005–2012* (London: Hurst, 2013), pp. 15–47.

[14] David M Anderson and Jacob McKnight, 'Kenya at War: Al Shabaab and its Enemies in Eastern Africa', *African Affairs* (Vol. 114, No. 454, 2015).

performs a crucial middleman role, trafficking vast quantities of ivory along a chain running through Somali ports to East Asian end markets.[15]

The media, NGOs and politicians have taken up both claims. The key source upon which they draw is a brief 2013 report by the California-based NGO Elephant Action League (EAL), entitled 'Africa's White Gold of Jihad'.[16] The outcome of an eighteen-month investigation, the report's headline assertion is that from 2010 to 2012 Al-Shabaab derived as much as 40 per cent of its running costs from trafficking Kenyan ivory (based on the estimated cost of paying 5,000 fighters $300 per month each). This figure rested on the claim that 1–3 tonnes of ivory flowed through Al-Shabaab-held territory *each month* – equal to $200,000–600,000 per month or $2.4–7.2 million per year.[17]

Numerous organisations and individuals have promulgated these assertions.[18] In 2013, the African Environmental Film Foundation launched the documentary *White Gold*, narrated by former US Secretary of State Hillary Clinton. The following year, US film director Kathryn Bigelow produced the short documentary film *Last Days*, linking ivory to Al-Shabaab's deadly 2013 attack on Nairobi's Westgate Shopping Mall.[19] At the initial screening of *Last Days* in September 2014, Peter Knights of WildAid – a supporter of the film – tellingly suggested: 'it's not about the facts, it's about the emotion'.[20]

Media outlets from *The New York Times* to *The Spectator*, the *Financial Times* and *New Scientist* have embraced the idea of an Al-Shabaab–ivory nexus.[21] Most have repeated the narrative without challenging it. A survey by the authors of online English-language stories published in 2011–15 by Western and East African outlets highlights 115

---

[15] On both claims, see Maguire and Haenlein, 'An Illusion of Complicity', pp. 5–11.

[16] Nir Kalron and Andrea Crosta, 'Africa's White Gold of Jihad: Al-Shabaab and Conflict Ivory', Elephant Action League, January 2013.

[17] *Ibid.*

[18] See, for example, International Fund for Animal Welfare (IFAW), 'Criminal Nature', pp. 12–13.

[19] African Environmental Film Foundation, *White Gold*, directed by Simon Trevor, 2013; Feeney, 'Premiere: Watch Kathryn Bigelow's Short Film about Elephant Poaching, Last Days'.

[20] Tristan McConnell, 'Illegal Ivory May Not Be Funding African Terror Group', *USA Today*, 14 November 2014.

[21] See Jeffrey Gettleman, 'Elephants Dying in Epic Frenzy as Ivory Fuels Wars and Profits', *New York Times*, 3 September 2012; Medina, 'The White Gold of Jihad'; Richard Schiffman, 'Ivory Poaching Funds Most War and Terrorism in Africa', *New Scientist*, 14 May 2014; Camilla Swift, 'How Al-Shabaab is Keeping the Black-Market African Ivory Trade Alive', *The Spectator*, 16 November 2013; Hillary Rodham Clinton and Chelsea Clinton, 'We All Have a Role to Play in Ending the Ivory Trade', *Financial Times*, 23 February 2014.

articles citing Al-Shabaab involvement in ivory trafficking. Only eight provided any critical commentary. Forty-eight used the EAL report as their main, and often only, source; sixteen relied on circular media reporting; and eighteen furnished no sources at all.

Meanwhile, politicians have furthered the narrative. In 2013, Kenyan President Uhuru Kenyatta announced that 'the money gained from the callous business [elephant poaching] is usually directed into funding terrorism'.[22] In 2014, Hillary Clinton wrote in a co-authored article for the *Financial Times*: 'We have seen al-Shabaab from Somalia, the Janjaweed from Sudan [and] ... the Lord's Resistance Army ... move into illegal wildlife trafficking'.[23]

Yet the evidence underpinning the Al-Shabaab–ivory narrative is limited. Indeed, rigorous primary and secondary research by the authors suggests that the extent of Al-Shabaab involvement in ivory poaching and trafficking has been significantly overstated.[24] Though impossible to rule out *any* Al-Shabaab involvement, this research suggests the existence of little more than small-scale, ad hoc and opportunistic participation. Notably, the primary source alluding to significantly greater involvement – the EAL's brief 2013 report – is plagued with methodological problems, which undermine its reliability, as discussed later in this chapter.[25]

With regard to poaching, a conflation of ethnic Somali poachers and Al-Shabaab is a common flaw in this and other efforts to show Al-Shabaab involvement.[26] Certainly, there is a history of Somali hunting dating back to the previous wave of poaching seen in the 1970s and 1980s. Yet this should in no way be taken as evidence of Al-Shabaab complicity today: ethnic Somalis are not necessarily or even likely linked to Al-Shabaab and may not even hail from Somalia, belonging instead to Kenya's large Somali diaspora. At the same time, recent research indicates a diversification in poaching profiles, with Borana, Turkana, Kikuyu and Meru individuals from communities surrounding Kenya's main rangelands increasingly attracted by the lucrative rewards on offer.[27]

---

22 Uhuru Kenyatta, 'The Path to Defeating the Al-Shabaab Terrorists', *Wall Street Journal*, 6 October 2013; Marc Nkwame, 'Tanzania: Uhuru – Poaching, Terror Linked', *Tanzania Daily News*, 26 March 2014.

23 Clinton and Clinton, 'We All Have a Role to Play in Ending the Ivory Trade'.

24 Maguire and Haenlein, 'An Illusion of Complicity'.

25 *Ibid*.

26 The Elephant Action League, for example, highlights the apprehension of 'Somali bandits' in 2007 to support a broader picture of Al-Shabaab participation in the ivory trade.

27 Authors' interview with community conservancy manager, Kenya, April 2015.

Geographical realities cast further doubt on claims of Al-Shabaab participation in poaching.[28] Kenya's largest elephant herds roam far from the Somali border, in Tsavo and Laikipia-Samburu.[29] Furthermore, DNA testing reveals that the majority of seized savannah elephant ivory is poached in areas even *less* accessible to Al-Shabaab, in the Ruaha-Rungwa and Selous-Niassa ecosystems of Tanzania and Mozambique. Since 2006, 86–93 per cent of large seizures (over 500 kg) globally surveyed by researchers at the University of Washington originated from herds in Selous-Niassa.[30] The physical distance between Al-Shabaab's base of operations and these ecosystems would appear to impede large-scale engagement in poaching in these areas. As for reserves close to the Somali border, reported Al-Shabaab presence in Boni and Arawale (as well as South Kitui further south) does not indicate large-scale involvement in poaching.[31] Although Arawale was linked to a rare, small-scale ivory seizure in Al-Shabaab-held territory in 2010,[32] surveys suggest that most elephants disappeared from these reserves as long ago as the early 2000s.[33]

Further difficulties arise around claims of an Al-Shabaab middleman role. The very viability of a major ivory trafficking route transiting Al-Shabaab-held territory in Somalia is questionable. It is not clear that pressure from enhanced law enforcement activity at ports such as Mombasa in Kenya in 2010–12 could have been sufficient to incentivise a circuitous, costly and risky Somali route as asserted by the EAL.[34] It is also unclear how the advantages of such a route could have offset costs arising from introducing an additional middleman – not least a high-profile terrorist group at the forefront of international scrutiny.[35]

No East African security studies expert has found evidence that Al-Shabaab earns large sums from ivory. Ivory does not feature in the

---

28 Maguire and Haenlein, 'An Illusion of Complicity', pp. 14–15.

29 Elephant populations are estimated at 11,000 in Tsavo and 7,000 in Laikipia-Samburu. See Elephant Database, 'Kenya: Provisional African Elephant Population Estimates', 2013.

30 Samuel K Wasser et al., 'Genetic Assignment of Large Seizures of Elephant Ivory Reveals Africa's Major Poaching Hotspots', *Science* (Vol. 349, No. 6243, July 2015), p. 85, Figure 4.

31 Jerome Starkey, 'Al-Shabaab Fighters Set Up Home in Elephant Reserve', *The Times*, 24 August 2015.

32 *The East African*, 'Militant Groups Fuel Poaching in East Africa', 14 October 2010; authors' interview with wildlife crime law enforcement officers, Nairobi, May 2015.

33 See Elephant Database, 'Kenya: Provisional African Elephant Population Estimates'.

34 Kalron and Crosta, 'Africa's White Gold of Jihad'.

35 Authors' interview with wildlife crime research consultant, Nairobi, July 2015.

analysis of scholars Stig Jarle Hansen, Christopher Anzalone and Matt Bryden, who have studied these questions for many years.[36] Nor has the UN Monitoring Group on Somalia and Eritrea found evidence of the movement of ivory, despite unearthing a wealth of evidence on other illicit goods transiting Somalia and monitoring the smuggling routes that would likely be used.[37] Meanwhile, not one large ivory seizure in transit or in destination ports has been traced to Somali ports, contrasting with frequent seizures linked to Mombasa in Kenya and Dar es Salaam in Tanzania.[38]

This lack of evidence of an Al-Shabaab middleman role is compounded by weaknesses in the methodology of the EAL report, as the main source attesting to such a role.[39] The report relies on a single Al-Shabaab source, without explaining where in the organisation this source stood. It does not state, for example, whether they were loosely affiliated to Al-Shabaab, and thus reliant on rumour, or whether they had first-hand knowledge of the group's ivory trafficking and its relative importance through a strategic position in the Maktabatu Maaliya, Al-Shabaab's 'ministry of finance'.[40] The source would have to be in a position such as the latter in order to paint a first-hand picture of everything from how Al-Shabaab sourced ivory from Kenyan brokers to how the group moved it out of Somali ports on charcoal-laden dhows for onward transport to East Asia.

The report also fails to place alleged ivory earnings in the context of Al-Shabaab's broader fundraising portfolio.[41] When compared with estimates of Al-Shabaab's total annual income – put at $70–100 million in 2011[42] – the $2.4–7.2 million figure cited in the EAL report appears much less significant than claimed, dwarfed by earnings from charcoal. Meanwhile, a monthly flow of 1–3 tonnes would equate to the ivory of

---

[36] Hansen, *Al-Shabaab in Somalia*; Matt Bryden, 'The Reinvention of Al-Shabaab: A Strategy of Choice or Necessity?', Center for Strategic and International Studies (CSIS), February 2014; Christopher Anzalone, 'The Rise and Decline of Al-Shabaab', *Turkish Review* (Vol. 4, No. 4, 2014).

[37] See, for example, Jarat Chopra et al., 'Report of the Monitoring Group on Somalia and Eritrea Pursuant to Security Council Resolution 2060 (2012): Somalia', 12 July 2013 (henceforth UNMGSE Report, 12 July 2013).

[38] Fiona M Underwood, Robert W Burn and Tom Milliken, 'Dissecting the Illegal Ivory Trade: An Analysis of Ivory Seizures Data', *PLOS One* (Vol. 8, No. 10, October 2013), pp. 1–12.

[39] See Maguire and Haenlein, 'An Illusion of Complicity', pp. 20–22.

[40] For information on the role of Al-Shabaab's Ministry of Finance, see Tom Keatinge, 'The Role of Finance in Defeating Al-Shabaab', *RUSI Whitehall Report* 2–14 (December 2014), pp. 9–10.

[41] *Ibid.*

[42] UNMGSE Report, 13 July 2012, p. 27.

1,200–4,700 poached elephants.[43] When compared to Kenya Wildlife Service poaching figures for the whole of 2012 (384 elephants, or roughly 2.9–3.8 tonnes of ivory), for example, it is clear that *all* the ivory poached in Kenya, as well as a large proportion from further afield, would have had to pass through Somalia to produce such figures. Such a scenario is highly unlikely given the market control this would demand relative to established crime groups using Kenyan and Tanzanian ports.[44] As for incomes, estimated monthly earnings of $200,000–600,000 from ivory are based on an average *sale* price and fail to account for what Al-Shabaab would have to *pay* to acquire Kenyan ivory. Finally, all of these figures assume *direct* Al-Shabaab control of the ivory supply chain, which is unlikely for an organisation that otherwise profits from trafficking by taxing other groups' operations.[45]

Taken together, these flaws in the EAL report – the source most commonly cited – and the lack of substantiating evidence cast doubt on the suggestion that ivory funds terrorism in East Africa on anything more than a small scale and on an ad hoc basis.[46] While there are occasional reports of very small amounts of ivory ending up in Kismaayo, Somalia,[47] the amounts involved represent little more than piecemeal evidence of potential small-scale movement of ivory at the most. Its existence merely casts further doubt on the existence of sizeable volumes transiting Somalia – or benefitting Al-Shabaab – without detection, despite UN monitoring.

The Janjaweed

There is greater evidence for involvement in ivory poaching and trafficking by both the Janjaweed and the LRA.[48] As a range of studies have started to

---

43 Based on an average tusk weight of 3.8–5 kg.

44 Christian Nellemann et al. (eds), *The Environmental Crime Crisis – Threats to Sustainable Development from Illegal Exploitation and Trade in Wildlife and Forest Resources* (Nairobi and Arendal: UN Environment Programme and GRID-Arendal, 2014), pp. 78–81; McConnell, 'Illegal Ivory May Not Be Funding African Terror Group'.

45 Authors' interview with director of research institute, Western diplomat, Nairobi, July 2015; Keatinge, 'The Role of Finance in Defeating Al-Shabaab'.

46 See Maguire and Haenlein, 'An Illusion of Complicity', p. ix; Nellemann et al. (eds), *The Environmental Crime Crisis*, pp. 78–81.

47 Authors' interview with director of private security firm, Nairobi, January 2015; authors' interview with senior environmental crime analyst, Washington, DC, July 2015.

48 Daniel Stiles, 'Ivory Trade, Terrorism and U.S. National Security: How Connected Are They?', <http://danstiles.org/publications/ivory/42.Ivory&National%20Security.pdf>, accessed 20 September 2016.

question the Al-Shabaab–ivory connection,[49] some politicians and NGOs have begun to avoid referring to Al-Shabaab, instead referencing solely the Janjaweed and LRA, alluding to a vague and unspecified notion of 'ivory-funded terrorism', or chopping and changing between organisations. In November 2013, Brooke Darby, deputy assistant secretary of state for the Bureau of International Narcotics and Law Enforcement Affairs, stated that wildlife trafficking could 'feed militant groups [and] terrorist groups'.[50] Six months later in the US Senate, she cited the LRA and Janjaweed as being involved in wildlife trafficking, avoiding mention of Al-Shabaab,[51] but a few months later referenced Al-Shabaab.[52] This chopping and changing reflects not just the unclear evidence behind such assertions, but also the confused political rhetoric around what these groups are, and what they represent.

Indeed, although there is broad consensus on the terrorist credentials of Al-Shabaab, the status of the LRA and Janjaweed as terrorist groups is disputed. Neither is designated a 'Foreign Terrorist Organization' by the US State Department,[53] yet both appear on terrorism databases such as the Terrorism Research and Analysis Consortium's database and the US National Counterterrorism Center's Counterterrorism Guide. In the case of the Janjaweed, an automatic application of the terrorist label represents a misunderstanding of the group's history, aims and objectives: the Janjaweed is not a group directly comparable to Al-Shabaab or the LRA.[54] Instead, it is an irregular militia formed from pastoral and nomadic Sudanese communities that have for centuries undertaken long-distance trade – whether in slaves, livestock or weapons – on horseback across Sudan, Chad, CAR and other Central African states.[55]

---

[49] See Jennifer G Cooke, 'Wildlife Poaching and Insecurity in Africa', CSIS, 14 July 2015; Diogo Veríssimo, 'Kathryn Bigelow and the Bogus Link Between Ivory and Terrorism', *The Conversation*, 16 January 2015; Jessica L Anderson, 'The Danger of False Narratives: Al-Shabaab's Faux Ivory Trade', *Africa in Transition*, blog of the, Council on Foreign Relations, 5 June 2015; Nellemann et al. (eds), *The Environmental Crime Crisis*, pp. 78–81.

[50] Mutambo, 'US State Department Links Poaching to Terrorism'.

[51] M Brooke Darby, 'The Escalating International Wildlife Trafficking Crisis: Ecological, Economic, and National Security Issues', statement before the Senate Foreign Relations Subcommittees on African Affairs and East Asian and Pacific Affairs, 21 May 2014.

[52] Anna Mulrine, 'To Combat Terror, Pentagon Should Help Fight Africa Poaching, Ex-General Says', *Christian Science Monitor*, 12 September 2014.

[53] US Department of State, Bureau of Counterterrorism, 'Foreign Terrorist Organizations'.

[54] Keith Somerville, *Africa's Long Road since Independence: The Many Histories of a Continent* (London: Hurst, 2015), pp. 251–52.

[55] *Ibid*.

Extensive research confirms this criminal-cum-trading orientation. The individuals that came to form the Janjaweed were a mix of pastoralist Arab clans from eastern Chad and Darfur, with Abbala Rizeigat at their core[56] – few of whom, prior to the 1980s, would have owned firearms. Yet as severe drought in 1984–85 sparked competition for resources, herders and farmers began arming themselves and the modern incarnation of the Janjaweed emerged as gunmen on horseback raiding farms and taking pastoral land by force.[57] Strengthened with arms provided by Libyan leader Muammar Qadafi in 1987–88, and from 1989 by Sudanese leader Omar Al-Bashir,[58] the Janjaweed nevertheless needed money and resources, having lost livestock in the drought. Benefiting from a steady supply of arms and ammunition, it found itself in a strong position to harvest and traffic ivory.

Reports of mounted Arab poachers crossing into the east of biodiversity-rich CAR to poach began to surface in the late 1980s, prior to reports of their movement further west and south, reaching northern DRC in the late 1990s.[59] This activity built on a longer history of cross-border operations; in written evidence to the US Senate Foreign Relations Committee in May 2012, WWF's Ginette Hemley and TRAFFIC's Tom Milliken noted the Janjaweed's association with criminal raiding and slave trading, aided by porous borders.[60]

Today, numerous sources have reported Janjaweed elephant poaching operations in locations across CAR, Chad, Cameroon and DRC. With regard to eastern CAR, the UN Panel of Experts for CAR has attributed responsibility for the area's decline in elephant numbers largely to Sudanese poachers.[61] International Crisis Group (ICG) interviews with CAR wildlife protection officers point to repeated dry-season forays into eastern CAR by groups of between 20 and 80 Sudanese poachers, operating on a large scale.[62] ICG

---

56 Alex de Waal, 'Who are the Darfurians? Arab and African Identities, Violence and External Engagement', *African Affairs* (Vol. 104, No. 415, April 2015).

57 Stiles, 'Ivory Trade, Terrorism and U.S. National Security'; Alex de Waal, 'Counter-Insurgency on the Cheap', *London Review of Books* (Vol. 26, No. 15, 2004).

58 Somerville, *Africa's Long Road since Independence*.

59 Stiles, 'Ivory Trade, Terrorism and U.S. National Security'.

60 Prepared statement by Ginette Hemley, senior vice president, Conservation Strategy and Science, WWF, and Tom Milliken, elephant and rhino leader, TRAFFIC for the Senate Foreign Relations Committee, hearing on 'Ivory and Insecurity: The Implications of Poaching in Africa', 24 May 2012, p. 54, <https://www.gpo.gov/fdsys/pkg/CHRG-112shrg76689/pdf/CHRG-112shrg76689.pdf>, accessed 19 September 2016.

61 See Louise Charbonneau, 'Sudanese Poachers Kill Elephants amid Central Africa Chaos: UN Experts', *Reuters*, 2 September 2015.

62 International Crisis Group (ICG), 'The Central African Crisis: From Predation to Stabilisation', Africa Report No. 219, June 2014, pp. 13–15.

research indicates that these poachers operate for their own profit, but also on behalf of Sudanese families with a history of ivory trading from the Nyala area of South Darfur.[63] There are also signs of collaboration with Sudanese army personnel, including discoveries of Sudanese army cartridges, uniforms and papers in Janjaweed poaching camps.[64]

Further afield, law enforcement officials suspect Janjaweed involvement in the killing of at least 300 elephants in Cameroon's Bouba Ndjida National Park in January 2012.[65] In March 2013, Arabic-speaking poachers on horseback slaughtered 89 elephants in Chad,[66] with the Janjaweed also accused of poaching in Dzanga Sangha Protected Areas, CAR, in May 2013.[67] In the weeks preceding these massacres, 28 poached elephant carcasses were discovered in Cameroon's Nki and Lobeke National Parks, with fifteen more found in four locations in CAR.[68] These incidents followed reports of bands of hundreds of Sudanese horseback poachers crossing CAR, heading for Cameroon and Chad.[69]

Conservationists and rangers have also reported Janjaweed operations in Garamba National Park in DRC. A study by conservation biologist Emmanuel de Merode and colleagues highlights reports from local communities and park wardens of poaching operations orchestrated by armed Arabic-speaking groups, including the Janjaweed.[70] Interviews conducted by the US-based NGO the Enough Project in 2015 with a range of local sources, including Garamba's chief warden, are consistent with these statements. These reports date Janjaweed operations in the park to 2004 and highlight evidence of Janjaweed presence as recently as February 2015.[71]

---

63 *Ibid*.

64 Julie Flint and Alex de Waal, *Darfur: A New History of a Long War* (London: Zed Books, 2008); Kasper Agger, 'Behind the Headlines: Drivers of Violence in the Central African Republic', Enough Project, May 2014.

65 CITES, 'CITES Secretary-General Expresses Grave Concern over Reports of Mass Elephant Killings in Cameroon', 28 February 2012.

66 *Phys.org*, 'Poachers Massacre 89 Elephants in Chad', 19 March 2013; IFAW, 'Killing Spree Slaughters 86 Elephants in Chad', 18 March 2013.

67 Peter Canby, 'Elephant Watch', *New Yorker*, 11 May 2015; Ledio Cakaj, 'Tusk Wars: Inside the LRA and the Bloody Business of Ivory', The Enough Project, October 2015; WWF, 'At Least 26 Elephants Massacred in World Heritage Site', 10 May 2013.

68 *CNN*, 'Cameroon Elephant Slaughter Latest in String of Killings', 27 March 2013.

69 IFAW, 'Criminal Nature'.

70 Emmanuel de Merode et al., 'Status of Elephant Populations in Garamba National Park, Democratic Republic of Congo, Late 2005', *Pachyderm* (No. 42, January 2007); K Hillman Smith and J A Ndey, 'Post-War Effects on the Rhinos and Elephants of Garamba National Park', *Pachyderm* (No. 39, 2005) pp. 106–10.

71 Cakaj, 'Tusk Wars', pp. 17–18.

Despite this, the extent to which ivory forms a major part of the Janjaweed's income is unclear. Scholars such as Gérard Prunier make no mention of ivory as a source of finance, attributing greatest importance to funding from Khartoum, income from food theft and cattle raiding, and the theft of aid from NGOs.[72] Julie Flint and Alex de Waal, in their comprehensive 2008 study *Darfur: A New History of a Long War*, discuss the economic importance to the Janjaweed of cattle and other livestock raiding, theft of food, abduction of people and ongoing Sudanese government subsidies, but make no mention of ivory.[73] It is also worth noting that the nature of Khartoum's ongoing support likely undermines the group's need to trade ivory directly for arms to continue its operations.[74]

Yet even more than this, it is the Janjaweed's problematic status as a terrorist group that undermines the support this case lends to a significant ivory–terrorism link. One of the most used descriptions of a terrorist organisation as one that seeks to 'intimidate governments or societies in the pursuit of goals that are generally political, religious, or ideological'[75] does not clearly apply to the Janjaweed, which is better described as a Baggara/Rizeigat criminal organisation-cum-trading network that hires itself out to the Sudanese army. Experts such as Daniel Stiles have emphasised their history as raiders, noting that the term 'Janjaweed' does not designate a 'movement' per se, but merely combines the Darfurian Arabic words for 'man', 'gun' and 'horse'. The term is commonly used in Sudan to describe a bandit or looter, and is devoid of political or ideological connotations.[76]

Indeed, the Janjaweed has not traditionally fought or sought to accumulate wealth for a specific political purpose, but simply as part of a diversified way of life. At times, this has involved fighting alongside the Sudanese army against the Sudan People's Liberation Army in the civil war that would eventually lead to the formation of South Sudan. At others, it has involved participation in the complex conflict in Darfur:[77] faced with insurgencies in the west and north, in the early 2000s Khartoum armed the Janjaweed, which fought as irregular units supporting Khartoum's army in return for arms, money and a licence to loot

[72] See Gérard Prunier, *Darfur: The Ambiguous Genocide* (London: Hurst, 2005), pp. 97–100.

[73] Flint and De Waal, *Darfur*, pp. 33–70.

[74] Stiles, 'Ivory Trade, Terrorism and U.S. National Security'.

[75] Joint Chiefs of Staff, Department of Defense, *Department of Defense Dictionary of Military and Associated Terms*.

[76] Stiles, 'Ivory Trade, Terrorism and U.S. National Security'.

[77] Jok Madut Jok, *War and Slavery in Sudan: The Ethnography of Political Violence* (Philadelphia, PA: University of Pennsylvania Press, 2001); Prunier, *Darfur*.

communities from which the government's enemies hailed.[78] The Janjaweed's government-sponsored operations in Darfur were internationally condemned, with rapes, killings and other abuses displacing more than 1 million in what the US subsequently labelled genocide.[79] Yet the Janjaweed's brutality does not automatically betray a political or ideological agenda. As one of the three principal groups cited as exemplars of ivory-funded terrorism, this therefore weakens the evidence underpinning a tusk–terror narrative.

The Lord's Resistance Army

A similar process of inconsistent labelling affects references to the LRA, as a third group commonly cited in support of an ivory–terrorism nexus. The LRA emerged in northern Uganda in 1987, the year after President Yoweri Museveni – then a rebel leader from southwestern Uganda – seized power, ending almost ten years of rule by leaders from the north.[80] Leader Joseph Kony established the group with the aim of defending and restoring the honour of his northern, ethnic Acholi people, and overthrowing Museveni.[81] Although the group's ideology has evolved over time, it was initially based on a spirit of rebellion – a group trying to overthrow those in power in response to a series of perceived injustices. This spirit of rebellion was combined with a unique blend of Christian and Acholi beliefs used to bond together recruits, legitimise the movement and create a code of conduct that would produce the perfect soldier.[82]

---

78 Julie Flint et al., 'Darfur Destroyed: Ethnic Cleansing by Government and Militia Forces in Western Sudan', *Human Rights Watch* (Vol. 16, No. 6(A), 2004).

79 Glenn Kessler and Colum Lynch, 'U.S. Calls Killings In Sudan Genocide: Khartoum and Arab Militias Are Responsible, Powell Says', *Washington Post*, 10 September 2004.

80 Ogenga Otunnu, 'Causes and Consequences of the War in Acholiland', Conciliation Resources, 2002.

81 Somerville, *Africa's Long Road since Independence*, pp. 260–63; Kevin C Dunn, 'The Lord's Resistance Army', *Review of African Political Economy* (Vol. 31, No. 99, 2004).

82 The blending of Acholi beliefs with aspects related to Catholicism has served as a bonding element for non-Acholi troops that joined the LRA, particularly the overwhelmingly Catholic Zande. See Philip Lancaster et al., 'Diagnostic Study of the Lord's Resistance Army', International Working Group on the LRA, June 2011, pp. 32–34; Kristof Titeca 'The Spiritual Order of the LRA', in Tim Allen and Koen Vlassenroot (eds), *The Lord's Resistance Army: Myth and Reality* (London: Zed Books, 2010), pp. 59–73; Joseph Kony quoted in Anthony Vinci, 'Existential Motivations in the Lord's Resistance Army's Continuing Conflict', *Studies in Conflict and Terrorism* (Vol. 30, No. 4, 2007), p. 342.

Kony proceeded to lead the LRA with astonishing brutality, condoning murder, torture, mutilation and rape – predominantly of his own Acholi people, whom he claimed had to be 'purified' through violence.[83] Since its formation, the LRA is thought to have caused over 100,000 deaths (although more certain numbers were not available until more recent years). The group caused massive internal displacement in northern Uganda between 1986 and 2007, whilst also expanding into Garamba National Park.[84] In 2008, the Ugandan military launched Operation *Lightning Thunder*, which helped to disperse the group across the wider region.[85] Since then, the LRA's fortunes have faded: today, the group is thought to number as few as 120 armed fighters,[86] scattered in mobile bands across parts of DRC, CAR and the Sudanese army-controlled Kafia Kingi – an enclave between Sudan and South Sudan.[87]

As with the Janjaweed, evidence of LRA involvement in ivory poaching and trafficking is more solid than in the case of Al-Shabaab. LRA operatives are known to have entered Garamba from 2005,[88] setting up bases and launching attacks, including on the park's head office in Nagero.[89] Rangers in Garamba provide testimony of poaching by the LRA; research by experts Philip Lancaster, Guillaume Lacaille and Ledio Cakaj provides further evidence of LRA operations in CAR and DRC parks, including Garamba.[90] Based on testimony from LRA defectors, further research in 2015 for the Enough Project suggests that ivory is poached in Garamba on Kony's orders and transported northwards, via southeastern CAR, to another LRA group, which moves the ivory into Kafia Kingi.[91] Here, it is thought to be sold to Sudanese merchants, often in exchange for food, ammunition or medicine.[92] Research by *National Geographic*, involving the planting of fake tusks embedded with a GPS tracking system

---

83 Somerville, *Africa's Long Road since Independence*.

84 UN Security Council, 'Report of the Secretary-General on the Activities of the United Nations Regional Office for Central Africa and on the Lord's Resistance Army-Affected Areas', S/2013/671, 14 November 2013, p. 11.

85 Alexis Arieff et al., 'The Lord's Resistance Army: The U.S. Response', Congressional Research Service, R42094, September 2015, p. 7.

86 Cakaj, 'Tusk Wars', pp. 4–8. Other recent estimates put the numbers of LRA fighters today in the low hundreds; see Arieff et al., 'The Lord's Resistance Army', pp. 1–3.

87 Small Arms Survey, Human Security Baseline Assessment (HSBA), 'The LRA in Kafia Kingi', October 2013.

88 Lancaster et al., 'Diagnostic Study of the Lord's Resistance Army', p. 23.

89 WildlifeDirect, '3 Still Missing After LRA Attack in Garamba', 22 January 2009.

90 Lancaster et al., 'Diagnostic Study of the Lord's Resistance Army', pp. 28–29.

91 Cakaj, 'Tusk Wars', pp. 7, 10–14.

92 *Ibid.*; The Resolve, 'The Kony Crossroads: President Obama's Chance to Define His Legacy on the LRA Crisis', August 2015.

in eastern CAR, revealed their movement along a route consistent with this – although, importantly, provides no evidence implicating the LRA specifically.[93]

However, the Enough Project's 2015 research, based on testimony from LRA defectors and prisoners, also suggests that the amounts of ivory involved are relatively small. It estimates that 38 tusks were poached and sold in 2012, with between 20 and 30 sold per year in 2013 and 2014 – approximately 100 pieces in total.[94] Of course, greater amounts may have been traded, of which the informants were unaware. However, testimony from other sources, including in Garamba, is consistent with these amounts, placing the LRA as a minor player in comparison to the large number of poaching gangs operating particularly from South Sudan.

The LRA's role in ivory trafficking should therefore not be overstated. Counts of tusks in the tens indicate a small-scale role in the global ivory trade, relative to the tusk counts that forensic analysis traces back to reserves such as Selous-Niassa in Tanzania/Mozambique.[95] Furthermore, the LRA is now weaker than ever before, dispersed across vast distances, with communication between its component parts inhibited by a bolstered African Union (AU)–US counter-LRA mission.[96] Reports of dissent and continuing defections cast doubt on Kony's ability to reverse the group's decline.[97] There are indications that this is having an impact on poaching operations. LRA groups are thought to have killed even fewer elephants in the last two years due to decreased manpower, military pressure from the AU–US force and a more effective response by Garamba rangers.[98]

Meanwhile, as with the Janjaweed, the group's status as a terrorist organisation is unclear, with implications for the support this case lends to the claim that ivory funds terrorism. Its classification has been inconsistent: the US State Department included the LRA on its Foreign Terrorist Organizations list in 2001 and labelled Kony a 'Specially Designated Global Terrorist' in 2008; yet the State Department subsequently downgraded the LRA, which does not appear today on its list of Foreign Terrorist Organizations.[99] As it was delisted by the US,

93 Bryan Christy, 'How Killing Elephants Finances Terror in Africa', *National Geographic*, 12 August 2015.

94 Cakaj, 'Tusk Wars', p. 12.

95 Wasser et al., 'Genetic Assignment of Large Seizures of Elephant Ivory Reveals Africa's Major Poaching Hotspots'.

96 The Resolve, 'The Kony Crossroads'.

97 Ledio Cakaj, 'Joseph Kony and Mutiny in the Lord's Resistance Army', *New Yorker*, 3 October 2015.

98 Cakaj, 'Tusk Wars', p. 10.

99 US Department of State, Bureau of Counterterrorism, 'Foreign Terrorist Organizations'.

however, the group was listed by others: the AU formally designated the LRA in November 2011, with the UN adding it to its Consolidated Security Council Sanction List as recently as March 2016.[100]

The LRA's inclusion on such lists has been questioned by scholars who suggest that the group was cast as a terrorist organisation from 2001 not because of a change in its character or activities, but because of a change in the geostrategic environment in which it found itself operating after 9/11.[101] In terms of its political agenda, it has been observed that in the early days this was constructed largely by external observers, based on a limited number of public statements by (alleged) members of the organisation.[102] Questions over the group's continued adherence to a political programme were raised further with the unravelling, in 2008, of the Juba peace talks, an internationally supported plan initiated in 2006 to end the conflict.[103] These saw the LRA compromise on what it was willing to accept politically, hinting at a less-than-steadfast adherence to a particular political position. Rather, immunity from prosecution by the International Criminal Court was one of the most (albeit not the only) prominent stumbling blocks.[104]

Debates around its designation aside, in light of its history of ivory trafficking, it appears that the LRA will continue, as long as it survives and is able, to use limited quantities of ivory as a means of obtaining food and other goods, including ammunition. However, its significantly reduced numbers, communications and logistics capabilities mean that it poses a localised rather than a major threat to elephant numbers. When considering further the questionable support provided by the case of the Janjaweed to the 'terrorism' narrative specifically, these two cases diminish the apparent role of terrorism in Central Africa. Add to this the limited evidence of involvement by Al-Shabaab in poaching in East Africa, and claims regarding terrorists' responsibility for the decimation of Africa's elephants appear unrealistic.

---

[100] US Department of State, 'The Lord's Resistance Army', fact sheet, 23 March 2012; UN, 'Consolidated United Nations Security Council Sanctions List', 1 November 2016; Aaron Maasho, 'African Union Declares Uganda's LRA a Terror Group', *Reuters*, 22 November 2011.

[101] Emma Leonard, 'The Lord's Resistance Army: An African Terrorist Group?', *Perspectives on Terrorism* (Vol. 4, No. 6, 2010).

[102] *Ibid.*; Sverker Finnström, *Living with Bad Surroundings: War, History, and Everyday Moments in Northern Uganda* (Durham and London: Duke University Press, 2008).

[103] For a detailed analysis of the Juba negotiations, see 'Part Three: Peace and Justice', in Tim Allen and Koen Vlassenroot (eds), *The Lord's Resistance Army – Myth and Reality* (London: Zed Books, 2010).

[104] *Ibid.*

Policy Implications

As in the case of CAR, explored in Chapter I with regard to an ivory–conflict connection, the reiteration of a significant ivory–terrorism link instinctively lends itself to calls for scaled-up enforcement-based responses. Such responses can present themselves as an effective means of both curbing poaching and countering terrorism. In 2014, Kenyan President Uhuru Kenyatta summarised this line of thinking when he declared that 'the war against poaching should be treated as a double-edged sword, which decimates two evils at once'.[105] Here, many of the same issues apply as those cited in Chapter I. First, where ivory forms only a minor component in an organisation's broader fundraising strategy, such approaches are likely to have only limited success. Second, where actors other than the target terrorist organisation have significant involvement in poaching, anti-poaching operations will not necessarily have a substantial impact on the latter's activities as their role may be secondary to other operators. This casts doubt on the wisdom of calls, including at the highest military and political levels,[106] for a strategy that relies on anti-poaching as an effective means to combat terror, in light of its ability to remove a key source of terrorism finance.

It is here that the greatest risk lies in terms of practical responses to the ivory–terrorism narrative. Indeed, the simplistic lumping together of diverse organisations implicated in this narrative, plus the horror and fear invoked by any atrocities they might carry out, gives these groups a prominence beyond their actual strength when it comes to ivory trafficking. In fact, these groups' relative share of responsibility for the wider volume of ivory that flows from source through transit regions and on to consumer markets appears to be minor in relation to that accounted for by organised criminal groups, as discussed in Chapter IV.[107] In the cases explored in this chapter, reliable evidence can link only relatively small amounts of ivory to these groups in the scheme of the vast quantities confiscated at various stages of the trafficking chain out of Africa. Despite the arguments about terrorist credentials, these groups are unlikely to account for even a significant minority of the ivory poached and exported from the continent since the onset, in the mid-2000s, of the current ivory trafficking crisis.

---

105 Nkwame, 'Tanzania: Uhuru – Poaching, Terror Linked'.

106 Mulrine, 'To Combat Terror, Pentagon Should Help Fight Africa Poaching, Ex-General Says'.

107 Maguire and Haenlein, 'An Illusion of Complicity'; Vanda Felbab-Brown, 'It's Corruption, Stupid: Terrorism, Wildlife Trafficking, and Obama's Africa Trip', Brookings Institution, 22 July 2015.

In light of this, it is concerning that the ivory–terrorism narrative has taken hold in the way that it has. This could speak in part to the interests this emotionally resonant imagery may serve. Often cited is a potential desire by some traditionally conservation-focused organisations to tap into the more significant funding associated with counterterrorism work. Similarly cited are the potential advantages offered by the arguably softer cloak of conservation to security agencies seeking to combat terrorism in fragile states (although it should be stressed that these remain as assumptions, with little evidence to substantiate them as motivating factors).[108] The greatest danger in all of this is that the fear invoked by an overblown ivory–terrorism narrative risks distracting attention and responses from where they would do best to focus. Mounting evidence suggests that the focus should lie on actors belonging to sophisticated, multilayered organised crime networks, the operations of which are facilitated by corrupt officials, as examined in Chapter IV.

108 Authors' interview with a Western diplomat, Nairobi, January 2015.

IV. POACHING, WILDLIFE TRAFFICKING AND ORGANISED CRIME

TIM WITTIG

One of the most serious security threats posed by poaching and wildlife trafficking may also be one of the least well documented: their relationship with organised crime. This goes beyond rhetoric on ivory as a conflict resource, and concerns poaching and wildlife trafficking as part of an organised environmental crime industry now considered by some analysts as the largest globally after trafficking in drugs and humans, and counterfeit crimes.[1] National governments and the international community now recognise the problem not only in environmental terms, but also as a serious emerging form of transnational organised crime.[2] Indeed, established organised crime networks appear to be increasingly engaging in wildlife crime as a lucrative – and still relatively low-risk – activity, and many African countries are facing convergence between wildlife trafficking and other forms of crime.

This chapter examines the relationship between poaching, wildlife trafficking and organised crime. It argues that this security dimension

---

1 Christian Nellemann et al. (eds), *The Environmental Crime Crisis – Threats to Sustainable Development from Illegal Exploitation and Trade in Wildlife and Forest Resources* (Nairobi and Arendal: UN Environment Programme and GRID-Arendal, 2014), p. 13. However, see the Introduction to this Whitehall Paper for difficulties with such calculations.

2 See, for example, European Commission, 'Communication from the Commission to the European Parliament, the Council, the European Economic and Social Committee and the Committee of the Regions: EU Action Plan against Wildlife Trafficking', 26 February 2016, <http://eur-lex.europa.eu/legal-content/EN/TXT/HTML/?uri=COM:2016:87:FIN&from=EN>, accessed 1 October 2016.

may be of greater concern than the relatively small amounts of ivory acquired by conflict and terrorist actors, as examined in Chapters II and III (although, as noted in Chapter II, the two threats may intersect). The exact nature of the organised crime threat remains poorly and largely only anecdotally documented. As a result, it is probably understated in political and media discourse on the security impacts of poaching and wildlife trafficking compared with that posed by militant non-state armed actors.

To shed light on the subject, this chapter analyses the most common narratives on the link between poaching, wildlife trafficking and organised crime – and the security threat this link poses in African source and transit countries. The focus is predominantly on higher-level wildlife trafficking beyond the poaching stage. Here, the chapter argues that the dominant narratives frequently assert the fact of organised criminal involvement without going as far as they might to consider its security implications. The chapter goes on to highlight a number of obstacles to addressing these security dimensions. It does so emphasising the stumbling blocks posed by a lack of understanding of the precise dynamics of wildlife trafficking and its overlaps with other forms of organised crime.

Beyond a Conservation Issue

As noted earlier in this Whitehall Paper, until the second decade of the twenty-first century, poaching and wildlife trafficking were viewed primarily in conservation and regulatory terms, even during the elephant poaching crisis of the 1980s and the early years of the current crisis, which began in the mid-2000s. Indeed, the 1980s crisis, which saw poaching-driven declines in elephant populations in many African range states comparable to those witnessed today,[3] was addressed primarily by a set of regulatory measures. These included a worldwide ban in 1989 on ivory trade that resulted in a collapse in the price of, and indeed the market for, ivory.[4] These measures were accompanied in some countries by special, targeted and finite enforcement operations to encourage compliance. However, poaching and wildlife trafficking remained fundamentally technical issues for conservationists and national wildlife and forestry authorities, rather than issues of significance for national or international law enforcement.

---

[3] See the Introduction to this Whitehall Paper for a more detailed discussion on quantifying declines in elephant populations as a result of the current poaching crisis.

[4] Andrew M Lemieux and Ronald V Clarke, 'The International Ban on Ivory Sales and its Effects on Elephant Poaching in Africa', *British Journal of Criminology* (Vol. 49, No. 4, 2009), pp. 451–71.

This has changed. Today, wildlife trafficking in particular has come to be understood not only as endangering the world's wildlife but also as an emerging organised crime threat, which warrants robust law enforcement interventions beyond established conservation and regulatory measures. The evolution of this understanding can be traced clearly through the legislation and policy instruments that have grown up in the last few years in response to wildlife trafficking. Increasingly, individual countries have sought to establish formally the status of wildlife trafficking as a serious form of transnational organised crime. The US, a leader in establishing robust institutional responses to wildlife trafficking, recognised the seriousness of the threat in 2013 when it established a Presidential Task Force on Wildlife Trafficking and issued a national strategy dedicated to combating such activity.[5] This was a notable development; as recently as 2011, the US government highlighted drug trafficking, trafficking in persons, cybercrime and weapons trafficking as serious organised crimes in its Strategy to Combat Transnational Organized Crime,[6] but omitted wildlife trafficking. The US has since been joined by the UK and a number of other countries in establishing initiatives and funding mechanisms to support robust responses to the issue.[7]

Such measures at the national level mirror increased attention to wildlife trafficking as an issue of organised crime within specialised international organisations and conservation NGOs. Many of these have increasingly (re)focused their work to highlight, and respond to, the threat posed by organised wildlife trafficking.[8] In 2010, the Convention on International Trade in Endangered Species of Wild Fauna and Flora (CITES) secretariat joined with INTERPOL, the UN Office on Drugs and Crime (UNODC), the World Bank, and the World Customs Organization (WCO) to form the International Consortium on Combating Wildlife Crime (ICCWC), a cooperative mechanism to build 'long-term capacity among national agencies responsible for wildlife law enforcement, and to provide

---

5 Barack Obama, 'Executive Order – Combating Wildlife Trafficking', White House, 1 July 2013.

6 National Security Council, 'Strategy to Combat Transnational Organized Crime', 25 July 2011, <https://www.whitehouse.gov/administration/eop/nsc/transnational-crime>, accessed 3 June 2016.

7 See, for example, the UK government's Illegal Wildlife Trade Challenge Fund, administered jointly by the Department for Environment, Food and Rural Affairs and the Department for International Development.

8 Marina Ratchford et al., *Criminal Nature: The Global Security Implications of the Illegal Wildlife Trade* (Yarmouth Port, MA: International Fund for Animal Welfare, 2013); Christian Nellemann et al. (eds), *Elephants in the Dust: The African Elephant Crisis* (Arendal: GRID-Arendal, 2013); Nellemann et al. (eds), *The Environmental Crime Crisis.*

these authorities with the tools and services that they need to combat wildlife crime effectively'.[9] Today, UNODC references nine separate UN resolutions, including two adopted by the Security Council, that provide it with international authority to combat wildlife trafficking.[10]

In April 2015, the UN Congress on Crime Prevention and Criminal Justice, held in Doha, Qatar, issued a formal declaration establishing priorities for addressing various types and drivers of transnational organised crime. This statement represented one of the first instances of formal UN recognition of wildlife trafficking as a serious form of transnational organised crime. The Doha Declaration included a section committing the international community 'To adopt effective measures to prevent and counter the serious problem of crimes that have an impact on the environment, such as trafficking in wildlife, including flora and fauna as protected by [CITES], timber and timber products and hazardous waste, as well as poaching'. They were called to do so 'by strengthening legislation, international cooperation, capacity-building, criminal justice responses and law enforcement efforts aimed at, inter alia, dealing with transnational organized crime, corruption and money-laundering linked to such crimes'.[11]

Following closely from the Doha Declaration, in July 2015, the UN General Assembly adopted its first-ever resolution on wildlife trafficking. The resolution recognises the status of 'illicit trafficking in protected species of wild fauna and flora' as 'an increasingly sophisticated form of transnational organized crime'.[12] It calls on member states to 'review and amend national legislation ... so that offences connected to the illegal wildlife trade are treated as predicate offences, as defined in the United Nations Convention against Transnational Organized Crime, for the purposes of domestic money-laundering offences'.[13] This followed on from World Wildlife Day 2015, themed 'It's time to get serious about wildlife crime', and dedicated in large part to exploring responses to wildlife trafficking as transnational organised crime. At the event, UNODC

---

[9] See CITES, 'ICCWC's Approach', <https://cites.org/prog/iccwc.php/Strategy>, accessed 6 August 2016.

[10] See UNODC, 'UNODC Legal Mandates for Wildlife and Forest Crime', <https://www.unodc.org/unodc/en/wildlife-and-forest-crime/mandates.html>, accessed 1 August 2016.

[11] UN, 'Draft Doha Declaration on Integrating Crime Prevention and Criminal Justice into the Wider United Nations Agenda to Address Social and Economic Challenges and to Promote the Rule of Law at the National and International Levels, and Public Participation', Paragraph 9(e), 31 March 2015.

[12] UN General Assembly, 'Resolution Adopted by the General Assembly on 30 July 2015', A/RES/69/314, 19 August 2015.

[13] *Ibid.*

Executive Director Yury Fedotov described wildlife trafficking as 'a transnational organized crime generating billions of dollars'. He spoke of the issue as 'an inter-generational crime' capable of 'permanently scar [ring] the world through the loss of some of our most beautiful creatures'.[14]

A consensus has thus developed among national and international policymakers, the conservation community, researchers and law enforcement bodies that wildlife trafficking is increasingly driven by transnational organised crime networks, and in itself represents a significant emerging organised crime threat at both national and global levels. As observed, this represents a notable evolution from previous thinking, which saw both poaching and wildlife trafficking primarily treated in technical conservation and regulatory terms, and largely excluded from the wider academic literature on criminology and organised crime (until recently, as the scale and sophistication of wildlife trafficking has increasingly been recognised).[15]

This agreement on viewing and responding to wildlife trafficking as a form of organised crime is an important development, especially in policy and political terms. However, it must be noted that this new consensus exists largely on superficial levels. Indeed, despite widespread acknowledgement in political and media discourse of the *fact* of organised criminal involvement in wildlife trafficking, there are few coherent, agreed-upon narratives on the precise *nature* of the organised criminal dynamics involved. In other words, while there is widespread agreement that wildlife trafficking represents both a serious conservation issue and an organised crime threat, there is only very partial empirical understanding of the precise dynamics of the relationship between organised crime and wildlife trafficking. There is thus limited analytic grounding for practical and policy responses. Addressing these gaps is critical.

Where CITES Ends and Organised Crime Begins

In assessing the evidence underpinning the intersection between wildlife trafficking and organised crime, it is helpful to consider briefly the history of organised, unregulated taking of wildlife and trade in derived products for profit. While such trade has long represented a threat to wildlife conservation and species survival, it is important to remember that it is and has not always been criminal. A review of this history is crucial to any

[14] UNODC, 'Organized Crime Threat to Wild Species on the Increase, Says UN on Wildlife Day', press release, 3 March 2015.

[15] Lemieux and Clarke, 'The International Ban on Ivory Sales and its Effects on Elephant Poaching in Africa'.

attempt to understand and ground the evidence available on today's organised criminal wildlife trafficking. This relates to the fact that the link between wildlife trafficking and organised crime – or crime in general – is a relatively recent phenomenon, inextricably linked with national and international efforts to control and limit the *legal* trade in wildlife.

Until the conservation movement took root in North America and Europe in the nineteenth and twentieth centuries, a range of species were regularly – and perfectly legally – hunted to extinction for economic reasons. Some, like the famous dodo (*Raphus cucullatus*), died out due to unsustainable hunting for meat and ostensibly to protect human settlements and livestock.[16] Others, in a direct antecedent to today's crisis, were pushed to extinction by organised, uncontrolled (but not, at the time, criminal) commercial exploitation. The great auk (*Pinguinus impennis*), hunted for its then valuable pelts, oils and feathers, became extinct in the mid-nineteenth century, with the last mating pair famously strangled to death on 3 July 1844 by two hunters, who also stomped on the last known egg of the species.[17] Similarly, Schomburgk's deer (*Rucervus schomburgki*) became extinct in the 1930s after decades of organised commercial hunting in its native forests of Thailand by those seeking to harvest its antlers for use in traditional medicine in Asia.[18]

Today, trade in wildlife and wildlife products continues to be a hugely profitable global industry, and perhaps under-appreciated among law enforcement and the general public is the fact that the vast majority of this trade remains legal. In 2009, for example, the legal trade in wildlife – encompassing everything from licensed species for the exotic pet trade to tradable reptile skins and mammal fur, to legal transfers of worked ivory produced before the worldwide ban in 1989 – was estimated, worldwide, to be worth around $370 billion.[19] In Europe alone, from 2005 to 2009, the trade in wildlife and derived products is estimated to have risen by about €7 billion, to a total of €100 billion in 2009.[20] CITES records for this period in Europe documented an average annual trade volume of more than 317,000 live birds, just over 2 million live reptiles, 2.5 million crocodilian

---

[16] International Union for Conservation of Nature (IUCN) Red List of Threatened Species 2016, '*Raphus cucullatus*', <http://www.iucnredlist.org/details/22690059/0>, accessed 1 September 2016.

[17] IUCN Red List of Threatened Species 2015, '*Pinguinus impennis*', <http://www.iucnredlist.org/details/22694856/0>, accessed 1 September 2016.

[18] J W Duckworth et al., '*Rucervus schomburgki*, Schomburgk's Deer', IUCN Red List of Threatened Species 2015, <http://www.iucnredlist.org/pdflink.79818502>, accessed 3 June 2016.

[19] TRAFFIC, 'Wildlife Trade', <http://www.traffic.org/trade/>, accessed 3 June 2016.

[20] *Ibid.*

skins, 1.5 million lizard skins, 2.1 million snake skins, 73 tonnes of caviar, 1.1 million coral pieces and nearly 20,000 hunting trophies.[21]

This large and ever-growing trade is regulated by CITES, which was signed in 1973 as the international community came together to ensure that legal trade was sustainable and did not lead to more species becoming extinct. The basis of CITES, as noted in the Introduction, is an internationally agreed list of protected species and various national and international-level laws and regulations to govern and control international wildlife trade. As an international treaty, CITES has been very successful: today, it is nearly universally ratified among UN member states, and serves as the foundation for a powerful and well-known international legal and regulatory regime, as well as associated national-level laws and policies aimed at ensuring the survival of more than 35,600 protected species.

CITES has also become the foundational international policy instrument against wildlife trafficking. It sets international rules and standards, and, through growing cooperation with international anti-crime organisations such as UNODC and INTERPOL, guides national governments in implementing more effective approaches to documenting and ultimately tackling wildlife trafficking. Yet here its record is more limited. Like any international convention, it has limits to its power, and while CITES is a crucial tool, fundamentally it is a treaty to control trade, not crime. In many ways, organised crime's involvement in the wildlife trade thus begins exactly where the power of CITES ends.

As an international trade treaty, CITES works through the power of legal and regulatory consensus and the national-level implementation of that consensus. In a practical sense, CITES forced not only national governments to change how they do business in regulating the trade in protected species, but also individual wildlife traders who were now subject to CITES regulations. Whereas in decades and centuries past wildlife traders could harvest and bring to market valuable wildlife-derived products just like any other tradable commodity, the emergence of CITES, CITES-based national laws and worldwide support for its principles and rules meant that those involved in wildlife trade had to adapt accordingly. Given the extensive legal trade today, it is clear that most wildlife traders adapted through compliance with requirements imposed on them by national laws and the international CITES regime, and also a realisation that sustainable legal trade is in their own long-term economic interest.

---

21 *Ibid.*

An unscrupulous minority of traders, however, have responded to CITES in the opposite way – through active non-compliance and the intentional, organised circumvention of relevant laws and regulations. Extensive evidence suggests that these specialised wildlife criminals maintain networks or links to networks that organise and commission the illegal taking (poaching) of CITES-protected wildlife at source locations; arrange and facilitate the illegal trade (trafficking) of these products across countries and international borders; and engage in wholesale and retail commerce with end users. The large volumes, long distances and complex supply chains involved indicate the participation of criminal enterprises operating with some amount of higher-level organisation. This is attested by numerous examples of seizures and, to a lesser extent, arrests along the supply chains used.

One notorious example of such organised and specialised wildlife criminal networks is the Xaysavang Network, allegedly run by Lao national Vixay Keosavang. The network has been implicated in a range of major seizures, including one in 2009 at Kenya's Jomo Kenyatta International Airport of 280 kg of ivory and 18 kg of rhino horn, originating from Mozambique and destined for Laos, worth an estimated $1 million.[22] The network's extensive involvement in fraudulently obtaining permits for rhino hunts in South Africa – and subsequently exporting and selling horns on the Southeast Asian black market – has been extensively documented by veteran wildlife trafficking investigator Julian Rademeyer.[23] Additional evidence obtained by Rademeyer and the NGO Freeland demonstrates involvement by the network in trading in pangolin scales, as well as in live animals, including rat snakes, monocellate cobras, king cobras, water monitors and endangered yellow-headed temple turtles.[24] In 2014, the US State Department offered a $1 million reward through its Transnational Organized Crime Rewards Program for information leading to the dismantling of the Xaysavang Network.[25]

The attractions of such activity for this and other organised criminal groups are clear. As a form of organised crime, trafficking in wildlife from,

---

22 Julian Rademeyer, *Killing for Profit: Exposing the Illegal Rhino Horn Trade* (Cape Town: Zebra Press, 2012), p. 296.

23 *Ibid.*, pp. 154–88, 288–99.

24 Environmental Investigation Agency (EIA), 'Untouchable? Wildlife Crime Kingpin Vixay Keosavang', 14 February 2014; Rademeyer, *Killing for Profit*, pp. 294–95; David Connett, '$1m Bounty on the "Pablo Escobar" of Animal Trafficking's Head', *The Independent*, 18 January 2014.

25 US State Department, 'Transnational Organized Crime Rewards Program: Xaysavang Network', <https://www.state.gov/j/inl/tocrewards/c60273.htm>, accessed 4 August 2016; EIA, 'Untouchable?'.

through and to CITES-signatory countries is easy and relatively low risk, with wildlife-related offences in almost all cases carrying significantly lower penalties and probability of arrest and prosecution than other forms of trafficking.[26] Evidence suggests that networks specialising in wildlife trafficking commonly manipulate CITES paperwork, as a low-risk strategy. This can include filing CITES forms for legally traded species to obscure trafficking in illegal ones, purchasing fraudulent paperwork from corrupt officials and laundering poached ivory using CITES-mandated paperwork that certifies it as legally traded ivory.

In one instance, a 2015 WildAid investigation on Hong Kong – the home of the world's largest legal ivory retail trade – uncovered widespread and open laundering of illegally poached ivory through the use of pre-CITES trading licences.[27] The investigation found that of 96 ivory traders surveyed in Hong Kong (about a quarter of the total in the city), only one was in full compliance with the law. While many of the violations cited by WildAid were apparently minor (including failing to properly display government-issued trading licences), anecdotal information from a 2015 WWF study appears to corroborate WildAid's findings.[28] In one secretly recorded conversation between a licensed ivory trader in Hong Kong and a WWF investigator posing as a buyer, the trader claims, 'I can buy smuggled ivory anytime ... I can send [it] ... to you from Africa'.[29] Another trader states that 'In general, if you are ordering (ivory) of less than 10 tonnes, I can sell it to you anytime. Some Hong Kong traders also buy ivory from us or they may import it themselves'.[30] This anecdotal evidence, combined with the fact that Hong Kong has long been a major transit hub for illegal ivory, indicates that likely a substantial percentage, even perhaps a large majority, of ostensibly legal ivory sold in the city is in fact illegal ivory smuggled into Hong Kong by criminal networks.[31] Of course, such manipulation of the boundaries between legal and illegal wildlife trade can also extend beyond international regulation to the exploitation of loopholes in national legislation. Examples here include the fraudulent use of rhino hunting permits seen in the Xaysavang Network's operations in South

---

26 Melanie Wellsmith, 'Wildlife Crime: The Problems of Enforcement', *European Journal on Criminal Policy and Research* (Vol. 17, No. 2, June 2011).

27 Peter Knights et al., 'The Illusion of Control: Hong Kong's "Legal" Ivory Trade', WildAid, 23 October 2015.

28 Cheryl Lo and Gavin Edwards, 'The Hard Truth: How Hong Kong's Ivory Trade is Fuelling Africa's Elephant Poaching Crisis', WWF-Hong Kong, 2015, p. 11.

29 *Ibid.*

30 *Ibid.*

31 Knights et al., 'The Illusion of Control'.

Africa, involving the recruitment of young Thai women to pose as hunters in sham hunts.[32]

The case of ivory presents perhaps the clearest picture of the scale of the facilitation of wildlife trafficking by sophisticated specialist organised crime groups. Here, global data from the Elephant Trade Information System, although affected by significant limitations such as an interdiction rate estimated at only 10 per cent,[33] reveals a picture of increasingly well-coordinated and organised trafficking. In particular, the rising number of 'large' illegal shipments of over 500 kg seized worldwide speaks clearly to the growing complexity and coordination of the trade, and to an increase in organised crime involvement – with CITES accepting 500 kg as an approved determinant of organised crime facilitation.[34] CITES data reveal that the frequency of such seizures has increased markedly since 2000, and especially this decade.[35] Prior to 2009, an average of five such events occurred annually, while in 2009–13 this rose to an average of fifteen.[36] Furthermore, in 2012–14, seizures of consignments of over 500 kg in weight accounted for 61 per cent of all ivory confiscated worldwide.[37] Here, specialised organised criminal coordination is signalled clearly by the inherent difficulties involved in consolidating the hundreds of tusks required to make up these volumes; in moving them across multiple borders along complex supply chains; and in avoiding interdiction at each stage – the latter also indicative of the corruption (both low and high level) that commonly oils the chain.

Not all organised criminal involvement in wildlife trafficking, however, is a function of the operations of large-scale, specialised networks. In parallel to these specialist wildlife traffickers, there is evidence to suggest that opportunistic entrants to the market, in the form

---

32 Rademeyer, *Killing for Profit*.

33 INTERPOL estimates that only around 10 per cent of illicit commodities are interdicted – an estimate widely applied to the ivory trade by NGOs, journalists and analysts.

34 CITES, 'Elephant Poaching and Ivory Smuggling Figures Released Today', press release, 13 June 2014.

35 CITES, 'Sixty-Fifth Meeting of the Standing Committee, Geneva (Switzerland), 7–11 July 2014: Elephant Conservation, Illegal Killing and Ivory Trade', secretariat report, SC65 Doc. 42.1, CITES CoP16, 2013, p. 28.

36 According to 2014 ETIS data. See Tom Milliken, *Illegal Trade in Ivory and Rhino Horn: An Assessment to Improve Law Enforcement Under the Wildlife TRAPS Project* (Cambridge: TRAFFIC International and USAID, 2014), pp. 5–6. For more information on the Elephant Trade Information System, see CITES, 'The Elephant Trade Information System (ETIS)', <https://cites.org/eng/prog/etis/index.php>, accessed 4 October 2016.

37 Samuel K Wasser et al., 'Genetic Assignment of Large Seizures of Elephant Ivory Reveals Africa's Major Poaching Hotspots', *Science* (Vol. 349, No. 6243, 2015), p. 85.

of existing local and transnational organised criminal groups, have sought to benefit from the relatively low risks and high rewards associated with wildlife trafficking. These actors range from local bushmeat-hunting gangs that turn their attention to poaching protected species such as elephant and rhino, to international smuggling networks already operating across source, transit or destination locations. The latter can make use of their existing logistical infrastructure to smuggle wildlife along with illegal narcotics, consumer goods and other contraband.

Such expansion is illustrated, for example, by the involvement of Chinese Triad gangs active in South Africa in trafficking of abalone, a large sea snail whose meat commands high prices in Asia. Since the 1990s, the Triads have been active in human trafficking, drug trafficking and other forms of organised criminal activity in South Africa, especially around Cape Town.[38] Although there is evidence of involvement in abalone trading in the 1990s, when its price spiked in around 2005 these gangs increasingly leveraged their criminal business connections in Hong Kong, Taiwan and mainland China to profit from this lucrative market.[39] In turn, they used their control of the abalone trade to broker arrangements with local gangs, in particular in the Cape Flats section of Cape Town, relating to the manufacture and distribution of Mandrax, the local name for a popular methamphetamine-based drug.[40] This saw abalone poaching and trafficking become closely intertwined with other forms of organised crime and indeed with the fortunes of poor communities for which abalone poaching offered a substantial income source. The result has been described as a coastal South Africa 'transformed from a network of small fishing communities, to outposts of international organized crime battling for the opportunity to harvest and export abalone'.[41]

Successful and sometimes well-known businesspeople also become criminal entrepreneurs as they seek to exploit the huge price differentials on illegal wildlife products between supply and demand markets. Meanwhile, corrupt officials are attracted to the significant rent-seeking opportunities available in facilitating wildlife trafficking activities. Illustrating this nexus between organised wildlife crime, corruption and business are two recent cases in Tanzania. In 2012, a member of Tanzania's parliament, Peter Msigwa, publicly accused the secretary-general of Tanzania's ruling party, Abdulrahman Kinana, of alleged

---

[38] Peter Gastrow, 'Triad Societies and Chinese Organised Crime in South Africa', Institute for Security Studies, Occasional Paper No. 48, 2001.

[39] International Union for Conservation of Nature (IUCN), 'The Disturbing War for Abalone', *National Geographic*, 8 December 2014.

[40] Sam Kiley, 'Rare Shellfish Bartered for Drugs', *The Guardian*, 23 September 2007.

[41] IUCN, 'The Disturbing War for Abalone'.

involvement in ivory trafficking.[42] Kinana is the owner of Sharaf Shipping, a company previously linked to a 2009 shipment of 6.2 tonnes of ivory seized in Vietnam.[43] Again relating to Tanzania, the Environmental Investigation Agency and *The Economist* both published the results of investigations into Mohsin M Abdallah Shein (also known as 'Sheni'), the owner of a transport business and various hunting blocks near the Selous Game Reserve, a donor to the Tanzanian ruling party, and a former member of its National Executive Committee. Mohsin has long been accused of alleged dubious hunting practices. Most recently he has been accused of allegedly using his political connections and substantial business interests in the country's safari and hunting industries to facilitate the illegal killing of perhaps thousands of elephants in southern Tanzania, especially in Selous.[44]

While not necessarily aligned with Hollywood-inspired perceptions of mafia-like organised criminals, most of these more opportunistic entrants to the illicit international market in wildlife likely fit with the definitions of transnational organised crime groups contained in the UN Convention against Transnational Organized Crime.[45] The convention – the most comprehensive legally binding global instrument for fighting transnational organised crime – specifies four defining features of transnational organised crime groups: they consist of three or more people who have not come together to form them randomly; they have existed for a period of time; they act with the aim of committing at least one crime punishable by at least four years' incarceration; and they operate primarily for the purpose of obtaining, directly or indirectly, a financial or other material benefit.[46] These characteristics clearly pertain to the majority of the groups operating in this illegal industry. The only notable exceptions to this – where organised crime is probably *not* a factor in wildlife trafficking – are in cases of human–wildlife conflict[47] leading to the ad hoc taking of individual animals and opportunistic, one-off trades, or alternatively in cases that occur in jurisdictions where penalties for wildlife trafficking do not meet the specified

---

[42] *The Economist*, 'Big Game Poachers', 8 November 2014.

[43] *Ibid.*

[44] *Ibid.*; EIA, 'Vanishing Point: Criminality, Corruption and the Devastation of Tanzania's Elephants', November 2014.

[45] UNODC, 'United Nations Convention against Transnational Organized Crime and the Protocols Thereto', 2004.

[46] *Ibid.*

[47] Human–wildlife conflict generally refers to interactions between wildlife and humans that result in negative human outcomes, such as loss of human life or property. For further discussion on this topic see, for example, Francine Madden, 'Creating Coexistence between Humans and Wildlife: Global Perspectives on Local Efforts to Address Human–Wildlife Conflict,' *Human Dimensions of Wildlife* (Vol. 9, 2004).

punishment threshold. While hard data are not available, neither of these two scenarios is likely to constitute a significant part of global wildlife trafficking as it is currently witnessed.

Meanwhile, corruption, as noted, is a known tool facilitating the operations of both specialist and opportunistic wildlife traffickers. Examples of corruption tied to poaching and wildlife trafficking in Africa are numerous and occur at all levels, from petty bribery of low-level field personnel to grand corruption involving government officials, up to ministerial and even presidential levels.

Taking East Africa as an example, recent years have seen a host of allegations, arrests and prosecutions relating to complicity of officials, from the lowest to the highest levels, in wildlife trafficking. To give just a few examples, in Kenya, a Kenya Revenue Authority officer, Lucy Kahoto, was arrested in 2015 in connection with the illegal exportation of 3,127 kg of ivory seized by Thai authorities in Bangkok.[48] Also implicated in the case was Siginon Freight, a company owned by the family of Kenya's former president, Daniel Arap Moi.[49] In Uganda, meanwhile, nearly a ton of ivory – worth an estimated $1.1 million – was discovered in 2014 to have gone missing from the Uganda Wildlife Authority's stockpile of confiscated ivory. This prompted an official investigation and has seen multiple news reports alleging collusion between corrupt officials and organised ivory traffickers, claims that have resurfaced at regular intervals.[50]

In Mozambique, a 2014 investigative report by the NGO Oxpeckers documented 'a web of official complicity' facilitating the illegal killing of elephants and trafficking of ivory in northern Mozambique.[51] This implicated by name administrative, judicial and tax agency officials in the northern provinces of Cabo Delgado and Niassa, exposed for involvement in the supply of high-calibre weapons to poachers, provision of access to protected areas and assistance in the export of ivory and rhino horn.[52] In Tanzania, in a 2012 speech in parliament, MP and former Minister of Natural Resources and Tourism Khamis Kagasheki accused four senior Tanzanian officials of allegedly facilitating ivory poaching and trafficking. These included Faith

---

[48] Philip Muyanga, 'KRA Officer among Six Charged over Sh576m Thai Ivory Haul', *Business Daily*, 23 June 2015.

[49] *The Star*, 'Moi Firm Siginon Linked to Sh570 Million Singapore Ivory Haul, Company Says it Loaded Tea Not Trophies', 21 May 2015.

[50] *The Guardian*, 'Ton of Ivory Missing from Ugandan Government Vault', 17 November 2014; Ronald Musoke, 'Uganda: Missing Ivory – Mutagamba Suspends UWA's Executive Director', *The Independent* (Kampala), 25 November 2014.

[51] Oxpeckers, 'Official Complicity in Mozambican Elephant Slaughter', 26 September 2014.

[52] *Ibid.*

Mitambo (MP for Liwale); Mariam Kasembe (MP for Masasi); Mtutura Abdallah Mtutara (MP for Tunduru South); and Vita Kawawa (MP for Namtumbo).[53] In 2012, the country's wildlife director, Obeid Mbangwa, and other top officials were dismissed for taking bribes for the assignment of hunting blocs and for arranging for more than 100 live animals to be flown to Qatar in 2010.[54]

These and a range of other prominent cases have seen corruption taken increasingly seriously as a facilitator of wildlife trafficking in African source countries. Meanwhile, a range of studies have sought to identify corruption risks along the value chain.[55] Indeed, there is now a fairly substantial body of literature linking corruption to wildlife trafficking, shedding light on additional cases and highlighting a range of methods involved. These range from the provision of critical information to poachers, to the supply of weaponry, the release of containers for export and the provision of high-level protection for trafficking operations.[56] In Zimbabwe, in a new method, an elephant-cyanide death scandal was in 2013 linked to top government officials and law enforcement agents.[57] In many such cases, however, investigations are quashed, evidence is removed or destroyed and no arrests or prosecutions are ever made.

The Threat from Organised Crime

The threat from the involvement of organised crime groups in wildlife trafficking thus exists at multiple levels, encompassing both powerful networks and a more grassroots component of smaller-scale, opportunistic criminals, facilitated by corrupt officials. In security terms, the threat from wildlife trafficking – and the corruption that helps to drive it – is comparable to that posed by other organised crime types. As noted by Peter Gastrow, the impact of organised crime on democracies, particularly in developing and weak states in Africa, is most damaging where criminal networks penetrate

---

53 EIA, 'Vanishing Point', p. 13.

54 Rhishja Cota-Larson, 'Tanzania: Wildlife Officials Fired for Animal Trafficking', *Annamiticus*, 15 August 2012.

55 Tanya Wyatt and Anh Ngoc Cao, 'Corruption and Wildlife Trafficking', U4 Issue (No. 11, May 2015).

56 *Ibid.* for a typology of corruption in wildlife trafficking, pp. 7–10, 13–14, 31–34; Tom Milliken and Jo Shaw, *The South Africa—Viet Nam Rhino Horn Trade Nexus: A Deadly Combination of Institutional Lapses, Corrupt Wildlife Industry Professionals and Asian Crime Syndicates* (Johannesburg: TRAFFIC, 2012); Maira Martini, 'Wildlife Crime and Corruption', U4 Expert Answer No. 367, 15 February 2013; Marceil Yeater, 'Corruption and Illegal Wildlife Trafficking', in UNODC, 'Corruption, Environment and the United Nations Convention Against Corruption', February 2012.

57 Caiphas Chimhete, 'Bigwigs Fingered in Hwange Elephant Poisoning', *The Standard*, 20 October 2013.

the political sphere to consolidate or expand their economic activities and to limit competition.[58] The impact has been described powerfully by Peter B Martin, and is as true today as when he originally penned it in 1999:

> Democracy around the globe is facing formidable challenges today, not from martial forces from outside, as we saw heretofore, but from subversive militants from within. Democracy is infected by a pernicious affliction initiated and propagated by organized crime that gains control progressively, maybe first as only a communal criminal gang, to later transform itself into a market driven force, eventually infiltrating the legitimate government at all levels, and finally rendering the government powerless.[59]

It is here that the likely explanation can be found for the difference in attention paid on the global stage to wildlife trafficking–security narratives linked to organised crime on the one hand, and those linked to conflict and terrorism on the other. While observers can easily grasp the more immediately frightening prospect of militant insurgent groups engaging in open warfare and attacks using funding from ivory, the threat posed by organised crime is more subtle. In a range of African countries, local, national and transnational criminal networks pose a threat to the state not through open confrontation but by quietly penetrating and subverting its institutions through bribery and corruption.[60] As observed by UNODC, 'organized criminals generally do not seek to topple the state, but they can provoke a reaction that can … threaten long-term peace prospects'.[61] Antonio Maria Costa, the agency's former executive director, notes further that 'transnational crime has become a threat to peace and development, even to the sovereignty of nations',[62] amounting at times to an attack on the foundations of the state itself – albeit one that is difficult to measure. In the words of Gastrow:

> The impact that this has on the state and its institutions is like slow biological warfare or radiation. It is hard to tell how much danger the state and its institutions are in at any given time. The poison or the effects of radiation accumulate and the impact may be delayed.

---

[58] Peter Gastrow, 'Termites at Work: Transnational Organized Crime and State Erosion in Kenya', International Peace Institute, September 2011.

[59] Peter B Martin, 'Confronting Transnational Organized Crime', in Emilio Viano (ed.), *Global Organized Crime and International Security* (Aldershot: Ashgate 1999), quoted in *ibid*., p. 2.

[60] Gastrow, 'Termites at Work', p. 1.

[61] UNODC, 'Crime and Instability: Case Studies of Transnational Threats', February 2010, p. 2.

[62] UNODC, 'Organized Crime Has Globalized and Turned into a Security Threat', press release, 17 June 2010.

> The infrastructure and the appearance of the institutions appear to remain intact, but there is a slow degeneration until it becomes clear that they have become so contaminated that they are no longer functional and unable to enforce their rules.[63]

The knock-on threats this can pose are significant: as organised crime eats away at governance and stability, countries can become locked in a vicious circle where social trust is lost and both rule of law and economic growth are undermined. At its most extreme, this process can undermine the credibility of domestic political systems and the social contract between citizens and their elected representatives, with potentially destabilising consequences where this intersects with existing grievances and governance problems.[64] Simultaneously, the process undercuts poverty alleviation efforts, as well as hollowing out national institutions, financial resource bases and the state's ability to provide public services.

It is very difficult to measure the exact extent to which organised wildlife trafficking currently contributes to these processes. This relates to the significant challenges in estimating the global size or value of wildlife trafficking, as explained in the Introduction to this Whitehall Paper. However, the elevated prices for wildlife products in destination markets and thus the substantial profits on offer suggests a powerful corrupting influence, in the form of significant sums available to buy compliance from law enforcement officers and politicians. The most frequently cited estimation of the revenues generated from global wildlife trafficking (comprising illegal trade in flora and fauna) is $7–23 billion.[65] Such significant sums would imply major criminal profit opportunities all along the trade chain that would have a commensurate, and broader, destabilising impact in the African source countries home to much of the wildlife in question.

In light of this threat, determined interventions are needed to stem the activities of the organised criminal networks driving it. However, numerous obstacles to effective responses remain. Most significant among these is an incomplete understanding – beset by a series of misperceptions and assumptions – of the nature of organised criminal involvement in poaching and wildlife trafficking itself. It is these misconceptions, and their impacts on efforts to curb poaching and wildlife trafficking and to minimise the threat to security, to which this chapter now turns.

---

[63] Gastrow, 'Termites at Work', p. 8.

[64] *Ibid*; UNODC, 'The Globalization of Crime: A Transnational Organized Crime Threat Assessment', 2010.

[65] Nellemann et al. (eds), *The Environmental Crime Crisis*, p. 19.

Knowledge Gaps as Impediments to Enforcement

In spite of the gravity of the threat posed, organised criminal involvement in wildlife trafficking is insufficiently understood. In a 2015 report, researchers Tom Maguire and Cathy Haenlein highlighted a range of knowledge gaps relating to organised crime and ivory trafficking in East Africa, all of which can be assumed to apply more broadly to other species and areas across the continent.[66] These gaps can be grouped into two core categories:

1. A lack of empirical knowledge and analytical understanding of the structure and operational dynamics of both 'higher-level' organised crime groups involved in wildlife trafficking and 'lower-level' organised crime networks which coordinate the procurement, transportation and consolidation of wildlife from source (poaching) locations to ports and transhipment hubs.
2. The extent of convergence between wildlife trafficking, corruption and other forms of transnational organised crime such as drugs, human and arms trafficking.

The persistence of these gaps in knowledge about the relationship between wildlife trafficking and organised crime should be seen in itself as a key issue of concern. After all, these knowledge gaps not only hinder a more comprehensive understanding of organised wildlife trafficking, but also undermine the ability to mount strategic, coordinated and effective interventions to combat the problem and the security threats linked to it. Indeed, if left unresolved, these knowledge gaps have the potential to unravel the emerging political consensus that addressing poaching and wildlife trafficking is worth the political and material investment in robust law enforcement responses.

This section discusses some of these gaps and their implications for understanding the relationship between poaching, wildlife trafficking and organised crime, and for attempts to address it. It does so first through examining the degree of hierarchical organisation of the groups involved. It does so second by examining the 'convergence question': the extent to which those organised crime groups involved in wildlife trafficking also take part in the trafficking of other illicit commodities. These discussions help us to consider the trajectory of the problem, on the basis of the

---

[66] Tom Maguire and Cathy Haenlein, 'An Illusion of Complicity: Terrorism and the Illegal Ivory Trade in East Africa', *RUSI Occasional Papers*, 21 September 2015. The assumption that these knowledge gaps can apply across other areas and species is based on the lack of any studies or analytic literature that explicitly contradict these findings for illicit trafficking of wildlife in other areas or in relation to other species.

evidence available, and ultimately the foundation of an effective strategy to counter organised criminal wildlife trafficking.

How Vertically Integrated are Wildlife Trafficking Networks?

An important point of tension exists between different perceptions of how wildlife trafficking networks are structured and how they behave. On the one hand, media reporting, public policy pronouncements and a number of well-known conservationists – where they go beyond the generalisations commonly put forth – tend to present a view of wildlife trafficking as being controlled by hierarchical, vertically integrated criminal groups led by a few powerful 'kingpins'.[67] On the other hand, virtually every detailed empirical study of wildlife trafficking networks, regardless of precise location or species, indicates a more complex reality in which smaller organised crime networks and individual facilitators work together within a diversified, horizontally integrated value chain for illegal wildlife products.[68] The 'kingpins', it turns out, may not always be the only or even the most important component of wildlife trafficking networks or criminal value chains. This question of vertical versus horizontal integration of the organised crime networks implicated in wildlife trafficking reflects a tension between public perception and observed reality, which threatens to undermine the effectiveness of strategies to curtail the activities of wildlife traffickers, as well as the public and political will necessary for such strategies to succeed over the longer term.

A number of examples illustrate a widespread bias towards the conception of wildlife trafficking networks as more vertically integrated than they may be in reality. For example, noted conservation scientist Samuel Wasser, in his February 2016 remarks to the American Association for the Advancement of Science, claimed that ivory trafficking in East Africa is controlled by a small number of powerful kingpins. He did so specifying that 'Probably one or two major dealers … are moving all of this ivory out of Mombasa, … the biggest transit area in Africa right now'.[69] This assertion was based not on reliable intelligence or empirical research into trafficking networks active in Mombasa, but on an assumption Wasser made in relation to his highly regarded DNA analysis of seized ivory, in which tusks from the same elephant often show up in separate shipments. This pattern

---

[67] *AFP*, 'Powerful Few Control Ivory Trafficking in Africa: Study', 15 February 2016.

[68] *Ibid.*; see also the case studies in Lorraine Elliott and William H Schaedla (eds), *Handbook of Transnational Environmental Crime* (Cheltenham: Edward Elgar, 2016); Varun Vira et al., 'Out of Africa: Mapping the Global Trade in Illicit Elephant Ivory', Born Free USA/C4ADS, August 2014.

[69] *AFP*, 'Powerful Few Control Ivory Trafficking in Africa'.

proved, according to Wasser, that the same powerful dealer must control the entire supply chain up to that point.[70]

A much simpler and more plausible scenario can also explain this phenomenon, however, which is also in line with existing research into wildlife trafficking networks in source and transit areas in Africa.[71] As an example, tusks from the same poached elephant could easily end up in separate export shipments if the illegal ivory trade in East Africa comprised multiple distinct criminal enterprises, some upstream, close to the source, and others downstream, close to the export hubs. For example, let us imagine an organised criminal poaching syndicate operating near one of East Africa's national parks. This gang and its backers primarily take 'orders' from one trusted ivory buyer for whom they regularly provide ivory, but also do business on various terms with other clients. In other words, while the gang may have a main customer that it presumably wants to keep happy, it is not fully controlled by it. Let us also assume that the buyer exports small amounts of ivory when possible, but also works with professional smuggling organisations capable of organising larger shipments, either hiring them as service providers to export ivory on its behalf or, at times, simply selling the ivory to these organisations, which in turn export it for their own profit. Because this poaching syndicate operates as a distinct enterprise from the higher-level buyer and export networks, it is entirely plausible that the syndicate may provide two different buyers – and thus supply two different shipments – with ivory from the same poaching operation or even the same elephant.

This example is hypothetical, but is similar to more recently documented dynamics of how poaching and local-level ivory smuggling networks operate. For instance, a recent 'carcass-to-port' geospatial analysis of ivory trafficking from the Ruaha-Katavi landscape in southern Tanzania, led by the author for the Wildlife Conservation Society (WCS), found that ivory trafficking in East Africa does not appear to be the product of any centralising mafia or transnational criminal organisation exercising control throughout the supply chain. Rather, the study found that ivory trafficking here is a diversified industry, characterised by opportunistic collaboration among localised criminal networks, commercial trade enterprises and corrupt officials.[72]

More specifically, the research found that ivory trafficking out of this particular landscape – one of the largest poaching hotspots identified in

---

[70] *Ibid.*

[71] See, for example, Vira et al., 'Out of Africa'.

[72] Wildlife Conservation Society (WCS), 'Ivory Trafficking from Southern Tanzania: A Carcass-to-Port Study', confidential final report to the Elephant Crisis Fund, 2016.

Wasser's DNA analysis of seized ivory – is the product of a five-layered business–criminal–political 'criminal ecosystem'. The first layer consists of poaching networks: semi-professional organised gangs operating in and around protected areas, comprising a combination of local villagers and higher-capability specialists, many of whom are non-local, experienced hunters or former soldiers. The second layer comprises upstream ivory procurement networks, which are usually politically connected and coordinate the acquisition, transportation and consolidation of ivory from upstream source locations to downstream ports and transhipment hubs with the aid of wider commodities or logistics-oriented businesses, such as transport companies and agricultural commodities dealers. A third layer consists of downstream logistics networks: politically connected export firms that coordinate the consolidation, shipment and onward international export of illegal ivory, often along with other commodities such as sugar, maize or fuel. The fourth layer is composed of the corrupt facilitators who secure government and private-sector assistance for the trafficking of ivory. The final layer consists of ad hoc opportunists: individuals and businesses facilitating all stages of the trade at the margins, whether local middlemen buying and selling small quantities of ivory they happen across, corrupt port officials taking advantage of situations presented to them to supplement their income, or small-scale exporters seeking extra profit by occasionally including a consignment of ivory in their regular activities.[73]

This organised criminal taxonomy echoes an earlier conceptualisation by Varun Vera, Thomas Ewing and Jackson Miller of the illegal ivory supply chain as a series of 'functional steps': collection; local transport (Africa); international freight transport; local transport (Asia); and processing. Each step, the authors argue, is 'centered at a different physical location, and entails the involvement of a wide range of actors'.[74] The report states:

> Each actor occupies a place in the value chain by virtue of the unique skills they bring to the table, and which increase in value with distance from the actual poaching. The more functional steps a network is able to control, the higher its level of vertical integration, and thus the higher its potential profit margin and the commensurate levels of organization and sophistication required.[75]

This latter observation is important. While vertical integration of each stage of the wildlife trafficking chain would indeed be highly profitable for a criminal network, achieving this is immensely difficult given the logistical

73 *Ibid.*
74 Vira et al., 'Out of Africa'.
75 *Ibid.*

and organisational challenges of exerting control at each step, across often vast distances and austere environments. No evidence is presented by these or other authors to indicate that such vertical integration actually occurs in any of the major ivory-sourcing hotspots. By comparison, there is significant evidence of vertical integration in other criminal supply chains, including the narcotics chain stretching from Latin America to the US. The US Drug Enforcement Administration, on the basis of this evidence, estimates that virtually all narcotics entering the US from Latin America are controlled by one of seven kingpin-led, vertically integrated organised criminal groups.[76]

Such vertical integration in relation to wildlife trafficking seems all the more unlikely given the mathematics of the cases of three individuals recently arrested in East Africa and labelled 'ivory kingpins'. These include Feisal Ali Mohammed (arrested in Tanzania and extradited to Kenya in December 2014); Abdurahman Mohammed Sheikh (arrested in Kenya in June 2015); and Yang Fenglan (arrested in Tanzania in September 2015).[77] Combined, these individuals are accused of exporting a total of 10.9 tons (9,888 kg) of ivory over the last decade, which according to recent scientific estimates of elephant tusk weight is equivalent to the ivory of around 1,500 elephants.[78] It can be assumed, however, that these kingpins were responsible for smuggling a larger amount of ivory than they have been formally charged with. As such, for the purposes of this example, let us increase this figure by a generous factor of ten, giving an estimate of nearly 15,000 elephant deaths for which these individuals are responsible. This sounds like a huge number, but by way of comparison, an estimated 100,000 elephants were poached in Central Africa in only the three years to 2014,[79] and Tanzania alone lost 65,700 in the period from 2009 to 2014,[80] to give the results of two recent surveys. As an approximate indication,

---

76 *Ibid.*; US Drug Enforcement Administration, '2015 National Drug Threat Assessment Summary', 2015, <http://www.dea.gov/docs/2015%20NDTA%20Report.pdf>, accessed 3 June 2016.

77 These individuals have been labelled 'ivory kingpins' by politicians, NGOs, analysts and journalists. See Willis Oketch and Joackim Bwana, 'Ivory Trafficking Kingpin Feisal Mohammed Jailed for 20 Years, Fined Sh20 Million', *Standard Digital*, 23 July 2016; David Smith, 'Chinese "Ivory Queen" Charged with Smuggling 706 Elephant Tusks', *The Guardian*, 8 October 2015; Weldon Kemboi, 'Police Arrest Mombasa Tycoon and His Two Sons over Ivory Seized in Singapore', *BarakaFM*, 4 June 2015.

78 Samuel K Wasser et al., 'Combating the Illegal Trade in African Elephant Ivory with DNA Forensics', *Conservation Biology* (Vol. 22, No. 4, 2008), pp. 1065–71.

79 George Wittemyer et al., 'Illegal Killing for Ivory Drives Global Decline in African Elephants', *PNAS* (Vol. 111, No. 36, 2014).

80 Karl Mathiesen, 'Tanzania Elephant Population Declined by 60% in Five Years, Census Reveals', *The Guardian*, 2 June 2015.

even with some very liberal assumptions, these three supposed kingpins are therefore responsible for smuggling only 10 per cent of Africa's ivory. This is likely to shrink to only 1 per cent (approximately) if the amounts cited by the authorities in the respective cases are nearer to the true amounts. In other words, as much as 90–99 per cent of Africa's ivory has been smuggled by people other than those acting within these three kingpin-led organised criminal networks. This suggests that rather than being true kingpins sitting atop a mafia-style, vertically integrated supply chain for ivory, these three alleged wildlife criminals simply belonged to organised crime networks involved in downstream logistics.

The Convergence Question

The range of functional stages involved in the wildlife trafficking chain is also relevant to the second question explored here: the extent of convergence between wildlife trafficking and other forms of organised crime. Again, this issue has crucial consequences for efforts to curb poaching and wildlife trafficking, and to address their security implications. Moving down the chain from the initial sourcing phase, many of the stages around consolidation, logistics and export are very close in nature to those required in other trafficking operations. The diverse functional skillsets used – from illegally sourcing a product to transporting it to export points, to circumventing export regulations – are not limited in their application to a model of smaller-scale wildlife trafficking networks cooperating horizontally. They are also relevant to an organisational model whereby organised crime groups of different types engage in the process: groups that are functionally specialised and diversified, with specialist areas such as logistics and export in demand, regardless of the precise commodity in question. Add to this the fact that wildlife trafficking in most CITES-signatory states is relatively low risk – in most cases carrying substantially lower penalties, as well as a lower probability of prosecution, than many other types of trafficking[81] – and the appeal of engagement by organised crime groups not traditionally associated with wildlife appears strong.

This is at odds with prevailing narratives around wildlife trafficking, and especially the tendency by governments, security agencies and international organisations, until recently, to treat wildlife trafficking separately from what they consider serious crimes. The tendency to silo wildlife offences, both conceptually and operationally, does little to encourage thinking about potential overlaps with other forms of transnational criminal activity.

This is a mistake. While a thorough discussion of all instances of wildlife trafficking and convergence with other crime types is beyond the

[81] Wellsmith, 'Wildlife Crime'.

scope of this chapter, recent research has highlighted a number of areas in which wildlife trafficking appears to be becoming deeply interlinked with other forms of transnational organised crime. These appear to pertain especially to international drugs trafficking and contraband smuggling. In South Africa, for example, illegal shipments of poached abalone are used as countervaluation for shipments of methamphetamines (known locally as Mandrax), as described above.[82] In East Africa, there appears to be substantial overlap between ivory trafficking and routes, individual smugglers and smuggling networks for heroin from Afghanistan and Pakistan, as well as for trafficking of cocaine, fuel and migrants from Somalia and Ethiopia, and illegal sugar and other agricultural commodities.[83] This is likely due to the opportunistic exploitation of existing smuggling infrastructure to transport and export ivory and other illegal wildlife products.

Policy Implications

All of this has implications for our ability to mitigate the security implications of wildlife trafficking. Indeed, the evidence seems to suggest, first, that wildlife trafficking is more accurately described as a value chain comprising numerous distinct organised crime networks working together both strategically and opportunistically. Second, it appears to suggest that these networks engage in multiple forms of criminality, making the problem more complex than the most commonly promoted narratives suggest. Though making the problem more complex, this more nuanced understanding also opens up important new avenues for targeting organised criminal networks involved in wildlife trafficking, and thus for reducing the security threat they pose.

Notably, the above analysis indicates that wildlife trafficking kingpins are only one set of actors in a range of other crucial organised criminal components within the trafficking chain, and in certain cases may not even be the most important targets for enforcement action. Arresting a few alleged wildlife-trafficking kingpins may be a useful symbolic tool for promoting the importance and feasibility of strong enforcement to the general public. However, it is not likely to be effective in actually saving protected wildlife, especially if done in isolation, as a horizontally integrated value chain can much more easily adapt to piecemeal targeting of ultimately replaceable individual nodes.

---

[82] *Mongabay*, 'Abalone Poaching Drives Meth Drug Trade in South Africa', 20 May 2007.

[83] WCS, 'Ivory Trafficking from Southern Tanzania'.

Such a value chain, however, is potentially more sensitive to disruptions of key logistical components; changes in the marketplace (for example, a drop in the price of the illegal commodity); or disruptions to the movement of illegal commodities between upstream (poaching and local transport) and downstream (export and wholesale) locations. This fits with recent research that has found that even more vertically integrated networks, such as drug trafficking organisations in Mexico, were most effectively countered by targeting not kingpins and other high-value individuals, but rather the specialist, harder-to-replace middle layers of the criminal network.[84] If the same holds true for wildlife trafficking, it could be most effective to target middle-layer organised criminal networks within the horizontally integrated criminal supply chain – and in particular those organised crime groups that work at the interface between upstream and downstream components, as well as those with important functional specialisms, such as logistical service providers, financial asset managers and experienced hunters. These middle layers are also potentially the most profitable levels at which to insert informers and undercover officers, as they have visibility over the operations and relationships of both lower-level (upstream) and higher-level (downstream) networks.[85]

Anti-wildlife trafficking efforts in line with this approach are already underway. For example, one highly successful yet underreported success was a series of strategically planned and well-executed raids in early 2015 by multiple government agencies targeting key middle-layer organised crime networks operating in the vicinity of Katavi National Park in Tanzania.[86] The raids targeted professional poaching gangs, small arms manufacturers and suppliers, and key logistics middlemen operating around twelve villages within the former Katumba refugee camp complex and known to be actively engaged in poaching, as well as trading ivory to organised criminals downstream.[87] The results of the raids were striking. Poaching declined shortly after the raids began and has stayed low ever since, likely because the targeting of these specialist middle layers in effect severs the relationship between upstream and downstream criminal networks and helps to de-professionalise the related criminal

[84] Vanda Felbab-Brown, 'Despite its Siren Song, High-Value Targeting Doesn't Fit All: Matching Interdiction Patterns to Specific Narcoterrorism and Organized-Crime Contexts', paper delivered at the Counter Narco-Terrorism and Drug Interdiction Conference, Miami, Florida, 16–19 September 2013.

[85] For further discussion of effective strategies for targeting criminal networks, see Paul A C Duijn et al., 'The Relative Ineffectiveness of Criminal Network Disruption', *Scientific Reports* (No. 4, February 2014).

[86] *The Citizen*, 'Special Report: Shocking Details Emerge as Secret Anti-Poaching Drive Takes Root', 30 March 2015.

[87] *Ibid*.

activity – perhaps disorganising organised crime.[88] The raids also demonstrated the efficacy of coordinated intelligence-led action involving multiple agencies. The operation around Katavi involved a number of Tanzanian enforcement agencies, including the National and Transnational Serious Crimes Investigations Unit, Tanzania Police Force, Tanzania People's Defence Force, Tanzania Intelligence and Security Service, Immigration Services Department, Tanzania National Parks Authority, and the Wildlife Division of the Ministry of National Resources and Tourism.

A multi-agency approach is also more effective due to the convergence between wildlife trafficking and other forms of transnational organised crime. Indeed, the opportunistic exploitation of existing smuggling infrastructure opens up further opportunities for enforcement and political action. Of particular note is the opportunity to engage counternarcotics authorities – which are generally more powerful than wildlife-related authorities – and counternarcotics operational units – which are generally more capable against complex trafficking networks – in taking action against drug traffickers who also trade in ivory. Externally funded and trained counternarcotics vetted units such as those operating in Kenya and Tanzania are highly capable and experienced in investigating and pursuing enforcement against complex and politically connected trafficking networks. The possible deployment of such units against common narcotics and wildlife trafficking targets merits exploration. Asset forfeiture is also a proven tool used against other transnational organised criminal networks that has not so far been commonly used against wildlife traffickers in Africa.

Four decades after the establishment of CITES, the world faces an organised, professional – and criminal – opposition not only to the convention's rules and regulations, but also to the fundamental principle that protecting endangered species is more important than the financial profits and materialistic enjoyment of a few people. The security threat this poses, to both individual citizens and the cohesion of the state, is understated relative to that invoked around ivory-fuelled conflict and terrorist actors; nevertheless, it is significant and demands urgent responses. Given the poor empirical documentation of this threat, building accurate and firmly evidenced understandings of the precise dynamics of organised crime-driven wildlife trafficking must be a priority for developing effective strategies and on-the-ground responses.

---

[88] Author interviews with conservationists in Kenya and Tanzania, September 2015 to February 2016.

CONCLUSIONS

CATHY HAENLEIN AND M L R SMITH

The world is currently dealing with a dramatic rise in poaching and wildlife trafficking that threatens to overturn decades of conservation gains. Yet today's wildlife trafficking crisis also threatens the security of human beings. It does so in ways often ignored by law enforcement and other security agencies slow to overcome institutional and mindset barriers to treating what has traditionally been labelled a 'conservation issue' as a serious crime with negative impacts on human wellbeing.

However, there are signs that this state of affairs is changing. Wildlife trafficking is no longer confined exclusively to the domain of wildlife authorities who are ill equipped to handle its complexities.[1] Although wildlife trafficking is still viewed in some source and transit countries as a regulatory issue best dealt with by park wardens, rangers and conservation scientists, in others it is increasingly incorporated into the purviews of security agencies.

This progress has come as the UN Security Council, alongside numerous other bodies, has acknowledged the links between poaching, wildlife trafficking, transnational organised crime and security. It has also occurred as major international donors have begun to take the security dimensions of poaching and wildlife trafficking more seriously. In 2013, the Clinton Global Initiative announced an $80-million action plan to combat poaching and wildlife trafficking, with particular emphasis on their security dimensions (although the Clinton Foundation itself provided no new funding, with the vast majority of the pledged funds comprising the already-funded budgets of a range of conservation organisations).[2]

---

1 Julian Rademeyer, 'Tipping Point: Transnational Organised Crime and the "War" on Poaching', Global Initiative against Transnational Organized Crime, July 2016, p. 10.

2 David Maxwell Braun, 'Global Partnership Formed to Save Elephants in Key Protected Areas', Voice for Elephants blog, *National Geographic*, 26 September 2013; Jane Edge, 'What Are NGOs Doing to Stop the Slaughter of Africa's Elephants?', *Africa Geographic*, 17 April 2015.

Following the 2014 London Declaration on the Illegal Wildlife Trade, the UK government committed to provide £13 million in new funding for projects addressing poaching, wildlife trafficking and their security ramifications, by developing sustainable livelihoods, reducing demand and strengthening the capacities of law enforcement and criminal justice systems.[3]

Where these and other sources of funding are targeted, along with the interventions they support, is a question that is crucial to their effectiveness. While sensationalist accounts of conflict actors and terrorists fuelling the global ivory trade may attract widespread attention, these actors are given greater prominence in public narratives than merited based on the evidence.[4] This risks diverting attention and funding from where they are most needed – notably from efforts to address the more pervasive influence of networked organised crime groups and the corruption that oils their operations.

In spite of this, some organisations may see a private interest in promoting the narrative that connects poaching, wildlife trafficking, conflict and terrorism. As noted by Jane Edge in relation to NGOs, some organisations may 'benefit from alarmist talk and every poaching outrage ensures an influx of funds into their coffers. However, responsible conservation should present considered facts and opinion; genuine action and accountability'.[5] Practical interventions will be effective only when carefully targeted at the levels, and at the groups, to which the greatest responsibility for the global trade accrues.

The sensationalist conflict–terrorism strand of the discourse has at times intersected with, and fed into, a parallel process of increasing militarisation of conservation practice in source areas, at the 'point of crime'. This has itself become a strand in discussions of the security implications of poaching and wildlife trafficking. Indeed, the more hardline responses predicated on conflict or terrorism narratives have contributed, in part, to the growing integration of biodiversity conservation initiatives and professional, militarised anti-poaching enforcement. This applies particularly to the protection of large and high-value pachyderms such as elephants and rhinos. In the case of South Africa, such a militarised outcome has occurred in the absence of a dominant terrorism narrative; rather, it has developed in response to what

---

3 Department for Environment, Food and Rural Affairs, 'Illegal Wildlife Trade (IWT) Challenge Fund', 4 August 2015, <https://www.gov.uk/government/collections/illegal-wildlife-trade-iwt-challenge-fund>, accessed 16 July 2016.

4 Tom Maguire and Cathy Haenlein, 'An Illusion of Complicity: Terrorism and the Illegal Ivory Trade in East Africa', *RUSI Occasional Papers* (September 2015).

5 Edge, 'What Are NGOs Doing to Stop the Slaughter of Africa's Elephants?'.

has been described as 'a declaration of war against South Africa by armed foreign criminals'.[6]

A number of voices have warned that militarisation can have dangerous consequences – including for the security of those living in and around source areas.[7] However, it is clear in today's world of well-equipped and armed poachers that some form of scaled-up anti-poaching enforcement is necessary. The question relates to balance: in the face of rapidly declining wildlife populations, to what extent should short-term protection trump longer-term prevention?

On the occasion of US President Barack Obama's historic visit to Kenya in July 2015, Brookings Institution Senior Fellow Vanda Felbab-Brown warned of the perils of an over-emphasis on militarisation in responding to poaching and wildlife trafficking, issuing a reminder that it is corruption and criminal activity that lies at the heart of the problem.[8] She did so noting that:

> [T]he thrust of [Obama's] engagement should not be principally on the misdirected over-securitization of wildlife conservation, which has involved a skewed and narrow focus on the role of militant groups in wildlife trafficking ... Instead, he should focus on issues of corruption among rangers, ecolodges, and often high-government officials and the participation of local communities in poaching. Without routing out this pervasive corruption and breaking the economic incentives of local communities to participate in or tolerate poaching, the bush wars will be lost, no matter how heavy the rangers' equipment.[9]

The section dedicated to elephant and rhino poaching in the *Small Arms Survey 2015: Weapons and the World* argues similarly that 'data supporting military anti-poaching policies is inconclusive'.[10] The report stresses that without parallel efforts to address the trade's drivers, efforts to deter poachers through armed interventions 'may *disrupt* poaching, but

[6] South African National Parks, 'Media Release: SANParks Enlists Retired Army General to Command Anti-Poaching', 12 December 2012.

[7] Daniel Stiles, 'The Ivory War: Militarised Tactics Won't Work', *The Conversation*, 9 November 2013; Zahra Moloo, 'Militarised Conservation Threatens DRC's Indigenous People: Part 1', *Inter Press Service*, 14 September 2016; Rosaleen Duffy, 'Waging a War to Save Biodiversity: The Rise of Militarized Conservation', *International Affairs* (Vol. 90, No. 4, July 2014).

[8] Vanda Felbab-Brown, 'It's Corruption, Stupid: Terrorism, Wildlife Trafficking, and Obama's Africa Trip', Brookings Institution, 22 July 2015

[9] *Ibid.*

[10] 'In the Line of Fire: Elephant and Rhino Poaching in Africa', in *Small Arms Survey 2015: Weapons and the World* (Cambridge: Cambridge University Press, 2015), p. 26.

[will] not stop it'.[11] The limitations of anti-poaching enforcement are also recognised by some of its staunchest advocates. In reference to rhino-horn poaching in South Africa, retired army Major General Johan Jooste, architect of South Africa's 'war on poaching', acknowledges that, though necessary, this is an unwinnable war. Ultimately, he states,

> Victory will not occur in the bush. You can do what you will ... but you're not going to win. The high demand ... means that poaching cannot be defeated with force on force. The only thing that can make a difference is taking on the crime networks. Victory will only occur in the courts.[12]

This points to a recurring theme in efforts to conceptualise poaching and wildlife trafficking as a security threat: namely, an uncertainty over whether to treat these phenomena as 'crime' or as 'war'. At the source end of the value chain, in the African bush, the phenomenon is frequently likened to a war – a 'war for wildlife' or a 'war on poaching'. This 'war', however, is ultimately a symptom of an emerging form of transnational organised crime. This type of organised crime responds to demand for wildlife products in distant locations, and therefore relies on the large-scale slaughter of wildlife.

It is here that the crux of the security dimensions of poaching and wildlife trafficking lies, and indeed here that the intersection of the various strands of threat examined in this Whitehall Paper – from human security to conflict, terrorism and organised crime – can be located. As illustrated by Felbab-Brown:

> [A]lthough fighters from ... [militant] groups might be the ones who pull the trigger, they are merely cogs in much larger wildlife smuggling networks who supply the demand, primarily in China and East Asia and among Asian diaspora communities around the world. A preoccupation with the militants without dismantling the larger smuggling networks and most importantly, without reducing demand for wildlife products – very difficult as that is, no doubt – guarantees failure.[13]

This reality is crucial to efforts to balance interventions aimed at addressing the security dimensions of poaching and wildlife trafficking. Whilst 'war' rhetoric around tales of bush-based rebel organisations slaughtering African elephants to fund attacks might loom large in the public imagination – thanks to sensationalist media reporting – in reality, the participation of militant groups is mainly at the lower ends of the value

---

[11] *Ibid.*, p. 7, emphasis added.
[12] Johan Jooste, quoted in Rademeyer, 'Tipping Point', p. 10.
[13] Felbab-Brown, 'It's Corruption, Stupid'.

chain and accounts only for a limited proportion of the wildlife poached and trafficked.[14] Their participation also predominantly relates to elephants, with little evidence linking conflict or terrorist actors to the numerous and lesser-known wildlife species affected by broader forms of poaching and trafficking. The actions of these groups, even in the limited areas where they play a role, are ultimately facilitated by a global supply chain continually amplified as criminals circumvent national and international controls, subverting attempts to distinguish legal wildlife trade from illegal wildlife trafficking.[15] As criminals undertake these activities, the networks they form and the endemic corruption they engender progressively penetrate the state – the start of a slippery slope towards the hollowing of national institutions. Governments that lack the capacity to counter such penetration, or that submit to it, risk morphing into criminalised or 'captured' states. In these states, development is held back, governance is undermined and public trust in institutions is broken down.[16]

The intention of this Whitehall Paper is thus not to minimise the seriousness of poaching and wildlife trafficking as security threats. The efforts made here to deconstruct certain narratives should not result in reduced concern for the impacts of poaching and wildlife trafficking on human populations in source and transit areas. Rather, the paper seeks to highlight an imbalance in media and political narratives: between a narrow focus on ivory as a driver of conflict and terrorism and the more insidious threats posed to state integrity, governance and human security by the organised crime and corruption that drive poaching and wildlife trafficking more broadly. The paper argues that this focus must be inverted. It does so stressing that the much-publicised potential role of insurgents and terrorists in poaching and wildlife trafficking is more of an exception to the overall scope of these phenomena than indicative of an emerging trend.

The threats posed to state integrity, governance and human security are closely linked to the fact that, despite organised crime groups' control of the value chain, local communities are commonly complicit in poaching. They may, for example, provide information on access routes or act as spotters and trackers. This can be the case even in community-run reserves, despite the rise of local ownership as the mantra of conservation. This links to the fact that the fate of such initiatives is

---

[14] Maguire and Haenlein, 'An Illusion of Complicity'; *Ibid*.

[15] See, for example, *BBC News*, 'Hong Kong Trade "Providing Cover for Smuggled Ivory"', 28 April 2016. See also Jackson Miller et al., 'Species of Crime: Typologies and Risk Metrics for Wildlife Trafficking', C4ADS, May 2015, p. 12.

[16] Peter Gastrow, 'Termites at Work: Transnational Organized Crime and State Erosion in Kenya', International Peace Institute, September 2011.

ultimately dictated by the strength of existing community leadership structures and the longer- or shorter-term economic horizons of community members.[17] As such, in addition to the multiple and complex political, social and economic factors driving this state of affairs, it is clear that good governance and the fight against corruption, at all levels, must form a core part of efforts to address poaching and wildlife trafficking. A holistic approach is needed to counter the different facets of the security threat posed – at the individual, regional and state levels. This must be based on a nuanced understanding of the inevitably diverse political, social and economic dynamics shaping the history of human–wildlife interaction and wildlife management in any particular location. This, in turn, must form part of a multidimensional approach to addressing the threat facing both wildlife and human populations.

This is an important point: in the past there has been a perception that the objectives of biodiversity conservation and development organisations do not align. Yet good governance is a common interest that unites their approaches. It is a component upon which both of their efforts inevitably rely, and indeed one which forms a basic principle in each of their approaches. Widespread and increasing corruption is a key enabler of poaching and wildlife trafficking as well as a significant obstacle to sustainable development. Efforts to curb it could and should therefore help to dissolve the unhelpful tension between those focused on development and those working on environmental protection.

There is evidence to suggest that corruption facilitates wildlife trafficking in a number of ways, at both the lower and higher levels.[18] As noted by NGO TRAFFIC's Director of Policy Sabri Zain, corruption 'threatens to undermine action against the organized criminal networks whose activities decimate wildlife and undermine good governance, the rule of law and the well-being of local communities'.[19] Whether as bribery of those tasked with defending wildlife, backhanders to policymakers or the falsification of export permits, corruption plays a persistent role in driving poaching and wildlife trafficking. At its most pervasive, this can see senior law enforcement officials or prosecutors – as well as politicians – bought into criminal networks.[20] As noted by Peter Gastrow:

---

[17] Felbab-Brown, 'It's Corruption, Stupid'.

[18] UN Office on Drugs and Crime, *World Wildlife Crime Report: Trafficking in Protected Species, 2016* (New York, NY: United Nations, 2016), p. 97.

[19] TRAFFIC, 'UK Spearheads Drive to Root out Corruption Fuelling Wildlife Crime', 11 May 2016.

[20] Jay S Albanese, *Transnational Crime and the 21st Century: Criminal Enterprise, Corruption, and Opportunity* (Oxford: Oxford University Press, 2011).

> This is corruption at its most dangerous ... the sophistication, and ability to corrupt with large amounts of money, is often confined to those involved in transnational organized crime networks. They are the ones who have moved up the social ladder and who mix with the elites because of their wealth, skills, and international exposure, and they are the ones who have the means to corrupt top figures in government.[21]

In the fight against the dual threat posed by corruption and organised crime, tools and lessons from all locations and forms of trafficking must be employed. In many source and transit countries, the fines or other punishments levied against poachers and wildlife traffickers are too small to act as an effective deterrent – reflecting the lack of seriousness with which this problem can still be treated. In many cases, the same applies to penalties for wildlife-related corruption. Where this is the case, it is essential that legislative frameworks are revised. As noted by criminologist Jay S Albanese, in order to be effective, the 'severity of the penalty associated with apprehension must outweigh the potential *gain* of the [criminal or] corrupt action'.[22] In many source and transit locations in Africa, in light of the significant profits to be made, a credible threat of incarceration, rather than fines, is crucial to effectively shifting the risk–reward calculus.

Closely linked to this is the tendency in many locations to treat seizures as an endpoint in investigations, with often limited efforts to go further to dismantle the networks driving poaching and wildlife trafficking.[23] In many source and transit countries, prosecution rates remain low; in many, no high-level traffickers have been successfully prosecuted.[24] At the same time, as noted by Julian Rademeyer, 'Borders, bureaucracy and a tangle of vastly different laws and legal jurisdictions are a boon to virulent and versatile transnational criminal networks and a bane to the law enforcement agencies rallied against them'.[25] In this context, more must be done to facilitate inter-agency, international and inter-regional cooperation and coordination, and to boost intelligence and investigative capacity. In addition, efforts must be made to strengthen the use of financial

---

21 Gastrow, 'Termites at Work', p. 8.

22 Albanese, *Transnational Crime and the 21st Century*. Emphasis added.

23 International Fund for Animal Welfare (IFAW), 'Singapore Ivory Seizure – Time to Move Beyond Seizures says IFAW', 3 April 2014.

24 As, until recently, was the case in Kenya: see Elizabeth Gitari et al., 'Outcome of Court Trials in the First Two Years of Implementation of the Wildlife Conservation & Management Act, 2013', WildlifeDirect Courtroom Monitoring Report 2014 and 2015, June 2016.

25 Rademeyer, 'Tipping Point', p. 4.

investigation tools, anti-money laundering and anti-corruption legislation in the investigation and prosecution of high-level wildlife crime.[26]

These efforts must be balanced, holistic and multifaceted – and they must take account of ongoing research into the dynamics of today's industrial-scale poaching and wildlife trafficking crisis. Where these efforts seek to address the security dimensions of poaching and wildlife trafficking, they must be based on a nuanced assessment of available evidence on the various dimensions of the threat posed: from its type, nature and magnitude, to the individuals and groups posing it, to the communities whose security is threatened. Here, as noted throughout this Whitehall Paper, knowledge gaps remain; the evidence available does not yet present a complete picture of the extent of the threat posed, in each of its manifestations. In this context, continuing research is needed. Only through a comprehensive and varied understanding of the evolving ways in which poaching and wildlife trafficking – and the responses to these activities – play out in specific locations can their security implications effectively be addressed.

These efforts to develop a more complete evidence base at source must be complemented all the way by determined efforts to reduce demand for wildlife and wildlife products in consumer markets. Ultimately, mitigation of the security threat posed by poaching and wildlife trafficking depends on concerted and effective interventions to address its demand-side drivers. As noted by the *Small Arms Survey 2015*, 'Without a substantial reduction in the demand for ivory and rhino horn, efforts to deter poachers ... may disrupt poaching, but [will] not stop it'.[27] Africa's wildlife population, including its many large mammal species, is part of what makes the continent unique, as a valuable source of natural and national heritage. Only by effectively addressing the market forces that sustain poaching and wildlife trafficking can we reduce the danger posed to this heritage, to endangered species, and also to humans who have suffered, or who could in the future suffer, as a result of the threats they present to our security.

---

[26] Tom Keatinge and Cathy Haenlein, 'Follow the Money: How Financial Investigation Can Combat Poaching in Kenya', *Newsweek*, 2 July 2016.

[27] 'In the Line of Fire', in *Small Arms Survey 2015*, p. 7.

About Whitehall Papers

The Whitehall Paper series provides in-depth studies of specific developments, issues or themes in the field of national and international defence and security. Three Whitehall Papers are published each year. They reflect the highest standards of original research and analysis, and are invaluable background material for specialists and policy makers alike.

About RUSI

The Royal United Services Institute (RUSI) is the world's oldest and the UK's leading defence and security think tank. Its mission is to inform, influence and enhance public debate on a safer and more stable world. RUSI is a research-led institute, producing independent, practical and innovative analysis to address today's complex challenges.

Since its foundation in 1831, RUSI has relied on its members to support its activities. Together with revenue from research, publications and conferences, RUSI has sustained its political independence for 185 years.

London | Brussels | Nairobi | Doha | Tokyo | Washington, DC